Y0-CKO-462

862.5
Bre
Fly

161729

Flynn.
Manuel Bretón de los Herreros.

**Learning Resources Center
Nazareth College of Rochester, N. Y.**

TWAYNE'S WORLD AUTHORS SERIES
A Survey of the World's Literature

SPAIN

Janet W. Díaz, *University of North Carolina at Chapel Hill*
Gerald Wade, *Vanderbilt University*

EDITORS

Manuel Bretón de los Herreros

TWAS 487

Manuel Bretón de los Herreros

MANUEL BRETÓN DE LOS HERREROS

By GERARD FLYNN
University of Wisconsin - Milwaukee

TWAYNE PUBLISHERS
A DIVISION OF G. K. HALL & CO., BOSTON

Copyright © 1978 by G. K. Hall & Co.
All Rights Reserved
First Printing

Library of Congress Cataloging in Publication Data

Flynn, Gerard C
  Manuel Bretón de los Herreros.

  (Twayne's world authors series ; TWAS 487 :
Spain)
    Bibliography: p. 159-65
    Includes index.
    1. Bretón de los Herreros, Manual, 1796-1873—
Criticism and interpretation.
PQ6506.Z5F55   862'.5   77-17498
ISBN 0-8057-6328-7

MANUFACTURED IN THE UNITED STATES OF AMERICA

To the Memory of
Emma and Wilkins Micawber

Contents

About the Author
Preface
Chronology
1. The Nineteenth Century Playwright — 13
2. The Early Theater: 1824–1833 — 23
3. Censorship and Several Plays of Bretón — 33
4. The Academy Speech and a Few Plays in Prose — 50
5. *Maroola* and Her Twin Sisters — 56
6. Figure, Coquetry, Gallantry, and Marriage — 68
7. Three Major Plays — 81
8. Bretón and the Drama — 103
9. The *Comediejas* — 114
10. Of Opuscules and Poetry: Tying Up Loose Ends — 121
Notes and References — 136
Selected Bibliography — 159
Index — 166

About the Author

Gerard Flynn is Professor of Spanish at the University of Wisconsin–Milwaukee. He first acquired a love for learning at the famous grammar school, P.S. 11, in his native Highbridge, The Bronx, New York. He believes that this school was the best one he has ever attended. The teachers there taught him to respect books, and years later he came to admire philosophy, history, and Spanish, in all of which he holds higher degrees.

Professor Flynn was born in 1924. He has published a volume on *Sor Juana Inés de la Cruz* and a volume on *Manuel Tamayo y Baus* (both Twayne's World Author Series), and a students' edition of Pío Baroja's *El árbol de la ciencia* (Appleton-Century-Crofts). He has also published articles on various literary subjects in professional journals.

Preface

The purpose of this book is to introduce the reader to the Spanish playwright Manuel Bretón de los Herreros (1796-1873). The first chapter emphasizes his biography, the following chapters his plays and dramatic theory, and the closing chapters his one act plays, poems, and essays. For insights into his life, I have relied on the books of his eminent biographer, the Marqués de Molíns, and of his most thorough critic, Georges Le Gentil. Few Spanish writers have received as fine a memorial as Molíns' *Manuel Bretón de los Herreros, recuerdos de su vida y de sus obras*.

The past criticism of Bretón falls roughly into two parts: nineteenth century essays, which consist largely of generalities, and the scholarly studies of the last thirty years, beginning with Charles B. Qualia's article of 1941 and Matilde López Serrano's *Berceo* articles of 1947 (see *Selected Bibliography*). Between these two temporal divisions fall Le Gentil's masterly work of 1909, the unfavorable criticism of Azorín in 1916, and the derogatory judgement of Carmen de Burgos in 1919. Azorín's adversely critical remarks, in line with the changing tastes of the public, may have helped to account for the paucity of comment in the decades preceding the Second World War.

I had hoped to include some original translations of Bretón in various appendixes, but considerations of space require their omission. To my knowledge, only one short play of his has been rendered into English, *Una de tantas,* with the title *One of Many* (consult Robert O'Brien's *Spanish Plays in English Translation*). As long ago as 1852, James Kennedy had translated fifteen pages of Bretón's poetry in his *Modern Poets and Poetry of Spain*. There is a French translation, *Le poil de la prairie* (1847), of *El pelo de la dehesa,* and Johannes Fastenrath rendered four of Bretón's plays into German in 1897.

A list of Bretón's plays will run to some 177 items, consisting of 103 original titles, 10 adaptations of seventeenth century *comedias,* and 64 translations, nearly all from the French. I have discussed about a third of the plays from this corpus.

MANUEL BRETÓN DE LOS HERREROS

Chapter 4 includes Bretón's Academy Speech of 1837, "Dramatic Literature: On the Use of Versification in Dramas." This succinct discourse will show why Bretón, a staunch advocate of versification in the theater, wrote all but five of his comedies in verse.

The *Selected Bibliography* recalls the comments of many critics of Bretón; the reader will find other comments in the text of this book and in the *Notes and References*. All the translations from Bretón's plays, poems, articles, and "opuscules" are mine; they cannot be found elsewhere. When making these translations, I omit the Spanish original unless the passage has some special lyrical value or other aspect worthy of recollection, such as a Gongorist line or a pun.

Most of the quotations in this book are taken from the five volume *Obras* of Bretón (Madrid: Imprenta de Miguel Ginesta, 1883-1884). *Obras 1883* is the reference for this collection. Volume and page are indicated thus: V, 342. Similar references are made for the other three major collections: *Teatro 1842* for the six volume edition of José María Lafragua (México: Imprenta de Vicente García Torres, 1842-1843); *Obras 1850* for the five volume edition published in Madrid by the Imprenta Nacional in 1850-1851; *Obras 1853* for the two volumes of the *Obras escogidas* (Paris: Baudry, 1853). These collections appear in the *Selected Bibliography*.

I owe several debts of gratitude: to my editors, Professors Gerald Wade and Janet Díaz, for their loyal criticism; to Señor Magallón of the Biblioteca Nacional in Madrid; to Mr. Alvaro Pérez and Mrs. Sabine Connerton, my students; to the ladies of the UWM Inter-library Loan, Mrs. Diane Cotter, Mrs. Merrilan Edwards, and Mrs. Janet Kennedy. Mrs. Winifred Baumeister took great care with the typing of these pages. I owe special thanks to my colleague of many years, Professor Pierre Ullman, whose knowledge of *Fígaro* and his era made him a reader of unusual capacities for the perusal of the manuscript.

GERARD FLYNN

University of Wisconsin-Milwaukee

Chronology

1796 December 18: Manuel Bretón de los Herreros born in the town of Quel, province of Logroño, La Rioja, Spain.
1806 His family moved to Madrid.
1808 The Napoleonic invasion of Spain.
1812 Bretón enlisted in the army.
1817 Wrote his first play, *A la vejez viruelas* (*The Young Old Codger*); not staged until 1824.
1818 Lost the sight of his left eye in mysterious circumstances.
1822 March 8: discharged from the army.
1823– His first decade in the theater, greatly influenced by
1833 Moratín.

1831 December 30: the première of *Marcela,* a turning point in Bretonian theater.
1834 October 23: the première of *Elena,* an attempt at Romantic drama.
1835– Quarrel and make-up with Mariano José de Larra.
1836
1835 April 27: première of *Mérope,* "a tragedy in three acts."
1836 July 5: première of *La redacción de un periódico (The Newspaper).*
1837 Married Doña Tomasa Andrés y Moya, his devoted wife until his death. The couple had no children.
1837 Entered the Spanish Royal Academy, reading his speech on "The Use of Versification in the Theater."
1837 April 27: première of *Muérete ¡y verás! (Die and You Will See),* which he considered his best play.
1838 October 26: première of *Flaquezas ministeriales (Foibles of State).*
1840 February 13: première of *El pelo de la dehesa (The Country Bumpkin).*
1842 January 13: première of *La batelera de Pasajes (The Ferry-Girl From Pasajes).*
1842– First published collection of Bretón's works: *Teatro,* six vol-

1843	umes, edited by José María Lafragua.
1843	May 3: première of *El editor responsable (The Editor Responsible)*.
1845	December 24: première of a one act play, *Frenología y magnetismo (Phrenology and Hypnotism)*.
1850	Appearance of the second collection of Bretón's works: *Obras,* five volumes, with a prologue by Hartzenbusch.
1853	Appearance of the third collection of Bretón's works, *Obras escogidas* (Paris: Baudry).
1867	January 16: his last play, *Los sentidos corporales (The Bodily Senses),* is staged.
1867–1873	An antisocial, bitter old age.
1873	November 8: death followed an illness of eight days.
1883	Publication of the famous biography of Bretón by the Marqués de Molíns.
1883	Appearance of the fourth collection of Bretón's works, *Obras,* five volumes, for which he had written a *Plan*.

CHAPTER 1

The Nineteenth Century Playwright

I *Introduction*

THE critics of Bretón's day often mentioned his comic verve (*vis cómica*) and Attic wit (*sal ática*).[1] He looked at the world with a twinkle in his eyes, or rather his one eye, and his jovial muse inspired him to speak humorously even of that infirmity:

> The Almighty left me,
> as a very special grace,
> exactly what I needed:
> two eyes for crying...
> and one alone to see with.[2]

He was a festive author who wrote scores of comedies about young people in love and old people interfering with them;[3] about masked balls, country homes, rival suitors, phrenology, the country bumpkin and the refined lady, the fat man in the small seat of a stagecoach, the ferry-girl and the army captain, the superiority of the country over the city or of city over country, a flirtation on a stagecoach, the live soldier taken for dead who learns on his resurrection which girl truly loves him, the question of who wears the pants in the family, mothers-in-law, gambling, dancing, soirées, wealthy men buying titles, the *ambigú* (buffet supper), the military, pretty girls, *cursi* (affected, tasteless) characters,[4] hypocrisy, false friendships, and dueling; but above all he wrote about love, in a joyous way. He himself may have grown sour in his last twenty years and become antisocial, but his plays never revealed that state of mind. Even his last comedy, *The Bodily Senses (Los sentidos corporales)*, written in 1867 when he was seventy-one years old, tells the love story of Angela and of Bruno, who finds both spiritual and physical beauty in his sweetheart. *The Bodily Senses* makes a suitably typical frame for the closing of Bretón's theater.

The critics of today have not taken so readily to Bretón's comic verve and wit, though they have not referred to him in so many words as a poor playwright.[5] One famous author, Azorín, has singled him out for special mention, admitting his comic talent but finding his comedies unsubstantial; they do not contain the ideal horizon (*lejanía ideal*) that Azorín, a competent novelist and essayist, professed to be seeking. Subsequent to Azorín's adversely critical remarks of 1916, and perhaps because of them,[6] Bretonian criticism has waned to the point where some revision is needed. It is hoped that the present book will partly fill this need.[7]

II *Quel: The First Ten Years (1796-1806)*

In a local color article called "The Stone Marriage" ("El matrimonio de piedra"), Bretón has this to say of his home town: "*Quel* (the time has come to say it), *Quel* is the name of my birthplace, worthy indeed of being honored with a less puny word, as we shall soon see. It is a pleasure to be the native of a polysyllabic town: one's mouth is filled with its name, and everybody understands when a person says, for example, I am from Casarabonela or Medinasidonia.[8]" In Quel, which sounds like "¿Qué?" ("What?", "How's that?"),[9] Manuel Bretón de los Herreros was born on December 18, 1796.[10] Both sides of his family enjoyed privileged social status, the names of Bretón and Herreros being listed on the parish register with an accompanying *Don*.

Quel is located in the province of Logroño, La Rioja, in the north of Spain. Famous for its vineyards, the area is dedicated to the wine industry, which dominates every phase of local life. At Bretón's birth his kinfolks, passing the leather flask around in celebration, had to go no farther than their own cellars to refill it. Bretón himself tells us that Quel, of two thousand people, was built around two huge rocks with wine vaults carved into them: "Some vaults are very spacious...; and it is noteworthy that although a middle-sized church suffices for the Savior's worship, with a sad little chapel annex out in the country, Bacchus has more temples there than he had in Greece." (Obras 1883, V, 529). This passage is typical of Bretón. Although he wrote it in 1855, when almost sixty years of age, his manner is playful and gay. He sees the lighter side of things. He shows no nostalgia or melancholy or attachment to

The Nineteenth Century Playwright 15

his home town and province, nor do his plays show such attachment. He is a full-fledged Madrilenian. Nevertheless, the first years of his life in La Rioja seem to have accounted for his peculiar talent of facile, humorous versification. It is said that the winedressers of Quel used to bandy couplets about and that the young Bretón, aged nine, was remembered for a witty quatrain.[11]

III *Madrid, The Napoleonic Invasion, Ferdinand VII (1806–1823)*

The year 1806 wrought a great change in the life of Bretón. His father, lured by the grandeur of Madrid and promise of preferment, mortgaged his vineyards and moved there with his wife and family of four children. Bretón attended the well-known school of the Piarists, the Escuela Pía de San Antón, as a day student. He studied Latin and Humanities until the school was suppressed by the French authorities in 1809; thereafter he studied independently with some of his teachers until 1811.[12] Perhaps the most important part of his Madrid education was simply his growing up there from age ten to almost sixteen. These years (1806–1812) saw the abdication of Charles IV, the flight of Ferdinand VII, and the arrival of Joseph I with a multitude of French reforms. The rustic boy from La Rioja was changed into a full-fledged citizen of Madrid.

One episode of this era left a deep impression on Bretón and may account for some of the bitterness of his old age. After his father died in 1811, leaving the family destitute, he went to an uncle for help but was rudely turned down. The refusal hurt him so profoundly that in 1825 he wrote his second original play around it, *The Two Nephews* or *School for Relatives* (*Los dos sobrinos;* see Act II, scene vii, of this play, where the young nephew, Cándido, insulted grossly by his aunt, replies to her).

On May 24, 1812, still fifteen years old, Bretón enlisted in the army.[13] This proved to be a momentous step in his life, for he stayed in the service until March 8, 1822, just two months short of ten years. His military experience shows up in many of his plays, for example, *The Ferry-Girl from Pasajes* (*La batalera de Pasajes,* 1842) and *Independence* (*La Independencia,* 1844). A common military scene is the *alojamiento,* the quartering of troops in civilian houses.[14]

The army years educated Bretón in many facets of Spanish life and indeed in Spain itself. He served with the *guerrilleros,* the infantry and cavalry. He marched through both Castiles, Catalonia, Andalusia, Valencia, and Murcia — he must have seen almost the entire country. He ate rice with saffron and soup with vinegar. He was lodged in rustic houses. He was smitten by "two Arab eyes," which became the source of his one act play *One More Coquette* (*Una de tantas,* 1837).[15] And during his army tenure, in 1818, he received a wound destroying his left eye and leaving a pronounced scar across his face. The circumstances surrounding the wound have been left in mystery by Bretón himself, who, when asked, used to give an enigmatic look and joke about it. Some critics argue that the wound came from a love affair and subsequent duel; in any case, owing to this grave injury, Bretón had a year's leave of absence from the army in 1818 and 1819.[16]

IV *A Theory of the Middle Class*

In one of his essays of local color (*artículos de costumbres*), Bretón speaks of the social classes in Spain. Since many of his plays deal with this class, and since he is an entertaining witness, he may once more be allowed to tell his own tale:

What we call the *lower class* has diminished in quality and quantity, just as the aristocracy has declined in wealth and authority. The middle classes are visibly absorbing the extreme classes, a phenomenon owing in part to the progress of civilization, in part to the influence of political institutions, whose advantages and disadvantages I don't propose to air here. The fact is you can no longer lay your eyes on those *chisperos* [low-brow dandies] whose sinister glance must still be remembered by a certain famous person of the court of Charles IV, nor those *manolas* [girls of flashy dress and sassy manners] who blessed with a two pound weight the soldiers of Murat who dared to make love to them.... Even in fashions, even when a person does not put on the *official* uniform that equalizes the rich man with the poor and the noble with the plebeian, there is a certain arbitrariness, a certain insubordination that is very much like anarchy. There is no longer a national dress for anyone, unless you look for it in some insignificant enclave of a town. We see more than one titled lord deck himself out in a sheepskin jacket and Andalusian hat, just as we see more than one common workman provide himself with a frock coat at the entrance to Mayor Street.[17]

Bretón, who wrote this passage in 1843, was obviously speaking of Fernandine and post-Fernandine Spain. In spite of Ferdinand's absolutism from 1823 to 1833, and perhaps even encouraged by it,[18] the middle class grew steadily in the early nineteenth century and became more and more the subject of literature. The playwright who best portrayed the middle class of the 1820s, 1830s, and 1840s was Manuel Bretón de los Herreros.[19]

V *The Early Theater*

Between 1824[20] and the death of Ferdinand VII on September 29, 1833, Bretón wrote and staged forty-six translations of foreign plays, mostly from the French of Molière, Racine, Marivaux, Scribe (thirteen by this French playwright), and others; eight modern arrangements (*refundiciones*) of Spanish Golden Age plays; and fifteen original plays, of which eight were major contributions.[21] He was obliged to write translations at the rate of approximately seven a year for economic reasons (*pro pane lucrando,* as he and his contemporaries frequently put it). The theaters paid very little for new material, and almost as much for a translation as an original. This practice was a source of complaint, and Bretón himself wrote in his preface to the 1850 edition of his works:

The reader will notice that original productions are not as plentiful in the first years of my dramatic career as in later years;... The cause of this apparent barrenness is as urgent as it is sorrowful. They paid very little for original works then, and to prove how miserable and precarious the situation of writers was I need only say that *A Madrid me vuelvo,* which during its first run lasted almost a straight month with a large sale of tickets, only brought me in a thousand *reales.*[22] ... They paid just a little less than that for translations, which are much easier to write and don't put the reputation of the author in jeopardy.[23]

The early original plays resemble the five comedies of Leandro Fernández de Moratín (1760-1828), the immortal *Inarco,* whom Bretón and all later playwrights admired. The story of *The Young Old Codger (A la vejez viruelas),* for example, Bretón's first play, is based on two of Moratín's comedies, *El viejo y la niña* and *El sí de las niñas,* and in keeping with the precedent set by Moratín, it is written in prose. In later life, Bretón used many rhyme schemes in his theater, but as a new playwright he used prose or the *redondillas* and *romances* prescribed by the master, Moratín.[24]

VI *The Turning Point:* Marcela

On New Year's Eve, 1831, the Madrid audience attended the

première of one of Bretón's most famous plays, and given the state of Spanish dramatic art at the time, it set a new standard in the theater. In the 1820s and 1830s, the stage presentations in Madrid consisted of Italian opera, translations and adaptations from the French, adaptations of seventeenth century Spanish plays, comedies of magic, gymnastic acts, spectacles and pantomimes, and a small number of new original Spanish plays.[25] As a critic, Bretón protested against the weakness of the Spanish stage; for example, he wrote one hundred thirty tercets, known as "The Philharmonic Mania," ridiculing the abuse of Italian opera in Madrid.[26] The best antidote he could prepare for a Spanish theater abounding in everything but original creations was a series of original creations of his own, such as his *Marcela* of 1831 and the many *comedias* that followed during the next two decades.

On January 2, 1832, Bretón wrote the review of his own play, *Marcela,* for the *Correo literario y mercantil.*[27] In the theater section, next to the title, he put the words "an original comedy in three acts, and written in various meters": here he was announcing the formal change from his previous comedies of 1824–1831 that was to become the hallmark of Bretonian theater. The comedies he had written previously were composed according to the precepts of Moratín, namely, in prose or octosyllabic verses with even lines in assonance (in Spanish, *romances*). The Moratinian formula was good for natural, rapid dialogue, but it prevented the use of other meters. Although Bretón never renounced his admiration for Moratín or his debt to him, beginning with *Marcela* he created his own comedy.[28] A pattern was emerging in his theatrical work: the first decade was Moratinian, the next decades Bretonian, and toward the end of his career, although still his own author, he wrote several plays paving the way for the *alta comedia* ("high comedy").[29] He also tried his hand at every genre the public relished: a Romantic play (*Elena*), a satire of Romanticism (*La ponchada* and *El plan de un drama*), tragedy (*Dido* and *Mérope*),[30] the comedy of magic (*La pluma prodigiosa*), one act plays, musical comedies (*zarzuelas*), and historical dramas (*Vellido Dolfos, Don Fernando el Emplazado,* and *Estaba de Dios*). In this sense he was eclectic.[31]

VII *The Height of His Career (1831–1846)*

As he approached middle age, Bretón, who had established himself as Madrid's first playwright, became a leading figure in its society. His activity during this period seems feverish. He had won the confidence of the two principal impresarios, José María Carnerero and Juan de Grimaldi, and the latter, director of the Príncipe theater, made him official poet of his company. He had joined the famous *Parnasillo* of the Príncipe cafe, where he associated with such young men as Patricio de la Escosura, Ventura de la Vega, Juan de la Pezuela, Mariano José de Larra, José de Espronceda, and the students of Alberto Lista, who became his lifelong friends. Living in Seville in 1830 with Grimaldi's company, he made the acquaintance of Mariano Roca de Togores, future Marqués de Molíns, and sometime before that he had met the Duke of Frías. His *Poems* were published in 1831. From 1831 to 1833 he took charge of the drama and music section of the *Correo literario y mercantil,* writing scores of articles; subsequently he wrote articles for other journals, the *Abeja* and the *Boletín de comercio.* In 1834 he resumed employment with the government, which had been interrupted in 1823, and in 1836 he became second librarian of the National Library (a sinecure not unlike a permanent fellowship). The new Athenaeum of 1835 took up much of his time, and the Lyceum, after it formalized its character in 1836, named him first counselor of the board. He worked hard at his tasks, since he was not one to take such a title as being merely honorific.

Bretón was active everywhere, in the theater, in the newspaper world, in cultural institutions, and in society. He was recognized and esteemed wherever he went, although he must have suffered from the barbs of carping critics, for he frequently mentions *aristarcos* and *zoilos* in his articles and even in his plays. (Aristarch was a famous critic of antiquity, and Zoilus was a malicious detractor of Homer and Plato; Bretón and his contemporaries used their names as common nouns.) One newspaper went so far as to call him *Brutón,* Big Brute, instead of *Bretón,* his family name.[32] It is the lot of famous men to suffer the envy of others.

For the biographer of Bretón, four events stand out in this period, each of which would merit a chapter in a full-length biography. The first is Bretón's quarrel with Mariano José de Larra (1809–1837), whose pen name was Fígaro, the most eminent critic and prose writer of his day. Thirteen years Larra's senior, Bretón had been a sponsor at the former's marriage in 1829, but by 1835–1836 the critic-playwright Larra and playwright-critic Bretón were engaged in a bitter quarrel; it is said that two of Bretón's plays are gibes at Larra — *I'm Leaving Madrid (Me voy de Madrid)* and *The Newspaper (La redacción de un periónico)*. Reconciliation came in July 1836, seven months before Larra's suicide, when at a gathering arranded by Molíns, Bretón improvised some peaceful verses ending with these words: "I in rancor overcame your, / You generously overcome me."[33]

The second event is his marriage in 1837 to Doña Tomasa Andrés y Moya. Bretón, who was forty years old at the time, made a wise choice, for he and his wife always remained devoted to each other. Although Bretón was anxious to have a family, the marriage was childless, and this may have subtly affected the bitterness of his old age.[34]

The third event is Bretón's entrance into the Royal Academy of Language, where he read his acceptance speech on June 15, 1837. His friend and future biographer, Molíns, had proposed him for membership, the Academy voted him a chair on June 8, and during the following week Molíns took him to see two illustrious academicians, the poet Manuel Quintana and the preceptor Alberto Lista. The latter had a portrait of Bretón on the wall with an epigraph of Ovid beneath, written in his own hand: *Et quot tentabat dicere, versus erat* ("And whatever he wanted to say, was in verse"). Possibly an inspiration for Bretón, possibly a coincidence, this epigraph contains the germ of his Academy acceptance speech, which argued that comedies are better written in verse than prose. The most remarkable part of the whole proceeding is the speed Bretón displayed in taking his chair: elected on June 8, he read his speech on June 15, just one week later! Bretón was an intense, industrious, sincere, ambitious man, with a most unusual drive. The festive nature of his comedies do not reveal this side of his character.[35]

The fourth memorable event of this period, the Carlist civil war of 1833-1839, deeply affected the lives of all Spaniards. Allusions to this strife constantly appear in Bretón's plays, and the plot of his personal favorite and most famous play, *Die and You Will See (Múerete ¡y verás!),* is based on the civil war itself; the protagonist, Pablo, goes off with the militia to fight the Carlists, is taken for dead, and returns to his own wake.[36]

This was a period of extraordinary achievement in the theater, for in just fourteen years (1833-1846), Bretón wrote sixty-five original plays. One can see the crescendo in his work by checking the catalogue of his nephew, Cándido Bretón y Orozco, in *Obras 1883,* I, and also the list of his works by the Marqués de Molíns. In

1833 there are, in chronological order, four translations, one modern adaptation (*refundición*), two translations, three original plays, one translation, and one original play. In 1834, 1835, and 1836, the pattern is similar. But in 1837 there is only one translation, and from that time until 1841, twenty-five original plays appeared in a row. The peak was 1843, with ten original works. This growth in original creations was owing in part to his economic well-being, for he no longer had to translate dozens of plays to earn a living; but it must be said that he used his new leisure for good hard work. To this period belong three of his four most famous plays (the other being *Marcela*): *Die and You Will See (Muérete ¡y verás!)*, *The Country Bumpkin (El pelo de la dehesa)* and *The Ferry-Girl From Pasajes (La batelera de Pasajes)*.

VIII Bitterness and Old Age (1846-1873)

In the 1840s Bretón's friends observed that he was becoming more gruff and disagreeable. Apparently many things contributed to this bitterness, for the evidence does not show a single cause. The critics who rejected many of his plays, calling them *sainetones* (pot boiler farces), left a psychic scar. After his play *The Punch (La ponchada)* was hissed by the offended militia, he was dropped from his office as second librarian, thus becoming a political *cesante*;[37] he always recalled this event with sorrow. In 1843 he experienced two saddening blows, the treachery of a friend and the death of his mother. In a letter to the Marqués de Molíns he wrote:

I have news for you of two misfortunes that have befallen me within a few days of each other. First, a person who made protests of friendship and whose reputation I respected has declared himself bankrupt and not in good faith according to well-founded reports. I had loaned him two thousand *duros,* my savings after so many years of hard work.

My second misfortune, though foreseen, is much more painful. My old mother died three weeks ago, and this irreparable blow might have done with me had Providence not given me a loving and consoling wife in my Tomasa, whose tenderness grows amidst my cares; she, the sweet and only link binding me to this truly miserable and reprobate world.[38]

When he wrote this letter Bretón was forty-six years old. Since he lived almost to the age of seventy-seven, one can glean from it an idea of his spiritual state in the last decades of his life. He became somewhat cynical of the goodness of most human beings and found consolation in the presence of his wife, a few relatives, and friends in the Academy and *tertulias* (get-togethers; at homes). It is remarkable that this acrimony did not sour his plays, which were still often festive, nor did it curtail his activity until his mid-seventies. In the last thirty years of his life he composed some two score plays and took on the demanding duties of director of the National Library and executive secretary of the Royal Academy.[39] He also received many other honors.[40]

Between 1870 and his death in 1873, Bretón became extremely antisocial. He ceased going to Academy meetings. He was still honored in many ways; for example, the emperor of Brazil visited him in his home and paid tribute to him as an equal, calling him "emperador del ingenio" ("emperor of the creative imagination"), but his condition remained unimproved. His chief pleasures were going over his old comedies and playing cards. Death came on November 8, 1873, after an illness of eight days.[41]

CHAPTER 2

The Early Theater: 1824–1833

THE "Emperor of the Creative Imagination," Don Manuel Bretón de los Herreros, most frequently wrote plays about young girls with pretty eyes who experience trouble marrying the young men of their dreams, betrothed to them by nature. These young girls dominate Bretón's early plays: in *The Young Old Codger (A la vejez viruelas)* the pretty eyes belong to Joaquina, in *The Two Nephews (Los dos sobrinos)* to Catalina; in *It's Back to Madrid For Me (A Madrid me vuelvo)* to Carmen, and in *The Phony Education (La falsa ilustración)* to Carolina. The other three plays of this period, *Gilding the Lie (Achaques a los vicios), The Frank and Candid Man (El ingenuo),* and *Marcela* have a somewhat different story to tell. *Love's Referee (Un tercero en discordia),* which is a companion piece to *Marcela,* returns to the theme identified with pretty eyes.

I The Young Old Codger (A la vejez viruelas, *1824*)

Bretón's early plays, which are comedies, belong to what Northrop Frye has called the low mimetic mode.¹ The heroes of these plays are neither superior to other men nor to their environment, and Bretón applies to them "the same canons of probability that we find in our own experience." When villains appear in search of gold, however, or when old people try to foil the amorous plans of the young, the comedies take on a decidedly ironic cast. Such is the case in *The Young Old Codger,* where we witness the frustration and absurdity of that aging beauty, Doña Francisca.

The Young Old Codger initiates a *senex* figure who reappears throughout Bretón's entire theater, even to his penultimate play, *Attorney for the Poor (El abogado de pobres,* 1866). The *senex*, or old man, is typical of the comedy of all eras and suggests the ritual origins of the genre. Figuratively speaking, summer, life, and fertility must battle against winter, death, and sterility, with the former winning in the end, often through a sudden happy ending: a young man overcomes the obstacles to his wedding placed there by his father. Young lovers stand at the heart of comic action, and repressive fathers (often mothers in Bretón) must be reduced to a state of permissiveness, as if the *senex* had to be sacrificed so that life might prevail.[2]

In *The Young Old Codger,* the old foolish person is the fifty-eight year old Doña Francisca, who prides herself on her great beauty. Wearing all kinds of wigs, with mattress padding under her corset, constantly admiring herself in the mirror, she is convinced that every young man she meets immediately falls in love with her. Consequently she knows that Don Enrique is her beau, whereas Enrique really loves her seventeen year old daughter, Joaquina, whom she has promised in marriage to a sexagenarian, Don Braulio. The cast is rounded off by Don Braulio's young daughter, Luisa, who loves her sweetheart, Don Mariano, in spite of her betrothal by her father to another man.

Prominent in this comedy are two moral ideas from the plays of Leandro Fernández de Moratín (1760-1828): old men should not marry young girls because nature has not designed their union, nor should young girls have their wills violated by heartless parents, who make them say yes. Of equal prominence with this moralistic teaching is the ridiculous figure of vain, old Doña Francisca, who sees herself as the heartbreaker of the opposite sex.[3] She is not alone in her conceit, for as Don Braulio explains in the closing sentence, she is but one of "all those vain, ridiculous and wanton old women who are the scorn and scandal of society." The play ends well, with Joaquina and Luisa marrying their true loves and with Don Braulio trying to bring Doña Francisca back to her senses.

The Young Old Codger, Bretón's first play, serves as a good introduction to the rest of his theater. Many of the ideas, actions, and modes of expression encountered there reappear frequently throughout the next forty years; here are several examples: Doña Francisca praises France, is abashed at Spain's awkwardness,[4] and drops many gallicisms, although she herself has never traveled beyond the Pyrenees. She speaks of good taste, but is herself hopelessly affected.[5] She is the *senex* figure who must be chastised so that young lovers can marry; indeed, the humor of this comedy is frequently based on age (e.g., if the sixty year old Don Braulio marries Doña Francisca's daughter, she will give him "the sweet name of son"). A comedy of errors takes place in which the language of various characters is misconstrued. The image of a man or a woman's *talle* (figure) appears, ridiculous in the case of Doña Francisca, admirable in the case of Don Enrique. There are many insights into social customs, for example, the possibility of a young girl's leaving her parents, taking asylum, and marrying without their permission.[6] And at the end of Act II, Don Braulio, ceding his claim to the hand of the young girl, plays the role of the *raisonneur* (the author's spokesman, who moralizes).[7]

The 1825 and 1850 editions of *The Young Old Codger* have somewhat different endings. The 1825 version refers to wanton old women who infest society, whereas the 1850 version speaks of wanton old women who are the scorn and scandal of society. The 1825 phrase records a fact that the 1850 phrase interprets: the bad example of old women may lead others into evil (scandal).[8] Perhaps the theological idea of scandal is the difference between a man's thoughts when he is fifty-four years old (Bretón in 1850) and when he is twenty-eight (Bretón in 1825). Or again, in 1850 Spain was on the eve of the *alta comedia,* with the moralizing dramas of Tamayo and López de Ayala, and Bretón's "scandal" is a precursor.

II The Two Nephews (Los dos sobrinos, *1825*), or, The School for Relatives

The two nephews are the innocent Don Cándido and the worthless Don Joaquín, who deceives his Uncles Marcelo and Onofre and his Aunt Juliana. These three vain, selfish people think Joaquín is wonderful and treat him well, whereas they scorn Cándido and speak to him as if he were a lackey. The young widow, Catalina, she of the beautiful eyes, also makes her appearance, as does Don Bruno, an aged, wealthy cousin. At play's end, Catalina will marry Cándido, and Don Bruno will be their protector.

Several elements appear in this play that were to become hallmarks of the theater of Bretón. First, the audience is introduced to the *viudita*, the beautiful young wealthy widow (Catalina), who is the object of many men's attention. Why was a young widow to become so prominent as a leading female role? The answer is multiple. Her widowhood accounts for her independence; she can say yes or no or simply try to attract a man without seeking the permission of a father, brother, or other male authority; in Bretón's play the widow is as free to select a male escort as a young girl of the

1970s. Her widowed state also accounts for her wealth, another incentive to marriage in Bretón's Madrid; her deceased husband was an older man with a fortune who died not long after their marriage. The young widow has a maturity most young women lack (e.g., Moratín's pliant females), and she understands the opposite sex, carefully judging the worth of a man. She easily rejects the advances of a flatterer like Joaquín and on the other hand knows how to attract the one person for her, in this case, Cándido.

The Two Nephews has a poetaster, who is a prototype of other Bretonian poetasters, such as Don Agapito in *Marcela* (1831). Joaquín, who has written a poem for Catalina, prides himself on such lyrical words as *pleonasm,* rhyming it with *sarcasm,* and *cantharides (cantáridas),* which he rhymes in Spanish with *arid (áridas)*! The girl's eyes are like two cantharides! Joaquín's sonnet is a study in what the Spanish call *ripios,* that is, word padding used to fill out verses or create rhymes (see Act I, scene vii).

The images of the coquette (*coqueta*) and of a beautiful figure (*talle*) that appear in this play will constantly reappear in Bretón's later comedies. There are several references to military life, some of which are explained in footnotes to the *Obras 1883* edition; for example, when a soldier says "I am no recruit, I already have the ninety," he means he has served more than twenty-five years, because men of such long service received ninety extra *reales* per month. Bretón was to refer to the military throughout his entire dramatic career.

But above all, as in most of Bretón's plays, there is the love story of a young man and woman. Love is a tyrant, and in love one always finds a certain discreet indiscretion:

CÁNDIDO:	Y usted, ¿qué motivo tiene para ponerse encarnada?	And you, what is your reason for blushing so?
CATALINA:	Usted se muere por mí y finge que no me ama.	You are dying for me, and pretend you love me not.
CÁNDIDO:	Y a usted quizá no le pesa, aunque finge que se enfada.	And perhaps you are untroubled, although you feign great fury.

(Act II, scene iii)[9]

III It's Back to Madrid for Me (A Madrid me vuelvo, *1828*)

In *It's Back to Madrid for Me,* the tyrannical provincial Don

The Early Theater: 1824-1833

Baltasar intends to marry his daughter Carmen to a rich country boor, Don Esteban. Carmen, another girl of the beautiful eyes, loves Don Felipe and would have to give him up were it not that her uncle, Don Bernardo, champions her cause against the *senex* figure, Esteban's mother. But in the end, as always in Bretón, young love wins out with the marriage of Felipe and Carmen.[10]

In form as well as plot *It's Back to Madrid for Me* adheres to the Moratinian model of *When a Girl Says Yes (El sí de las niñas.)* Bretón, like Moratín, observes the three unities of time, place, and action. The play starts at seven in the morning and ends at nightfall,[11] with the tight conflict taking place "in a lower room of Don Baltasar's house." Bretón summarizes the unity of action in one speech of Carmen's:

> How critical, how terrible
> my situation! If I accept
> Don Esteban as my spouse,
> I hasten my sad end;
> refusing him, I plunge
> a dagger in my father's breast. (Act II, scene i)

Each of the three acts rhymes in assonance, the first in *a-e,* the second in *e-a,* and the third in *e-o.* Unity in the rhyme scheme was inherited from eighteenth century Neoclassicism.

Bretón, however, sensed the need for variety[12] in his theater and introduced some diversions. The play begins with the Madrilenian Don Bernardo's praise of country life:

> Here the air
> is fresher; the customs
> more simple; here no one
> is looked up to
> except the priest and mayor; (Act I, scene iv)

The theme of "scorn of city and praise of country",[13] dating back at least to the sixteenth century, is given an odd twist by Bretón that accounts for the title of his comedy. At the play's end Don Bernardo says:

> I deny it not;
> but I had formed
> another judgement of the country.

> I thought that all was peace
> there, candor and virtue.
> Ah! the best book is
> experience; so says the refrain.
> Here sordid envy
> sits upon its throne;
> here the voice of nature
> is kept in brutal silence.
> ....
> How awful! It's Back to Madrid for Me!
> where more comforts may be found
> though vices are not fewer.

The reader also encounters a generous use of Spanish idioms and proverbs — for example, "le dan vela en este entierro?" ("Is this any of your business?"); "esto pasa de castaño oscuro" ("This is the limit"); "yo la haré entrar por vereda" ("I'll set her straight"); "todos no están cortados por una misma tijera" ("they're not all cut of the same cloth"); "quien bien ama, tarde olvida" ("True love never forgets, come sunshine or rain"). One *costumbrista* speech of Bernardo's describes the Prado in Madrid:

> How much better is the Prado!
> Where people show off their dress,
> where intrigues are made,
> and dances planned,
> and a man can court the girls
> and outwit their mothers;
> a person censures those behind,
> and steps on those ahead.
> Your attention is caught
> by that beautiful figure [*talle*]
> in which nature moans
> the victim of art;
> now you see the hair of Belisa....,
> who owes it to some cadaver;
> now the fairness of Anarda
> which white cream[14] enhances.
> Who alights from that carriage?
> The Marquesa of Ensanche,[15]
> a seamstress of yesteryear.
> And who that madcap
> humming between his teeth
> an aria from *Mercadante,*

> who goes about greeting all
> though he doesn't know a soul?
> He's an innkeeper's son
> who came here from Flanders,
> and giving chalk for cheese[16]
> made himself quite the man.
> What a Babylon! What dust!
> What a striking contrast
> those fine braids
> and short dress coat
> make with the filthy rags
> of the unkempt rogue
> who goes about selling taper lights!
> And the coaches' noise,
> the hubbub of the people,
> the continuous rubbing of shoulders
> and next to the statue of Apollo, the muse,
> creator of the arts!
> that battalion of horses,
> so prosaic, so unglorious....
> Ugh! that's enough. Just thinking
> of it makes my flesh creep. (Act I, scene iv)

In the 1820s a stroll along the *paseos* ("promenades") was the favorite pastime of Madrid. "The best known promenade, because its fame went back more than a century and a half, was the Prado,"[17] whose pleasures Bretón burlesques in the previous passage.

In one speech, Don Baltasar refers to the Old Christian lineage of Esteban, a boast still of moment in the 1820s (an "Old Christian" was a person descended from Christians, with no known mixture of Moorish, Jewish or heathen blood); he also mentions the nineteenth century, "this infamous century," a reference that later Bretonian characters would often repeat. The citizens of the nineteenth century were both fascinated and repelled by the momentous changes of their era, for although they admired the general progress, they were wary of changes in manners.

IV The Phony Education (La falsa ilustración, *1830*)

The plot resembles Moratín's *El viejo y la niña* and Molière's *Tartuffe*. Don Fabricio, a romantic swindler, has won the confidence of Doña Mamerta and her daughter, Carolina, who has been reading "immoral books." He turns their heads; they are all for modern enlightenment and for rejecting traditional values such as home and family. But the good sense of Carolina's relatives and beau (Don Luis) wins out in the end, and the swindler is exposed. The latter's wife arrives in Madrid like a deus ex machina, and he must go to jail. Carolina will spend a year making amends and then marry Luis.

Although *The Phony Education* was by no means one of Bretón's better plays, it is important nevertheless in a study of the present kind. Ordinarily Bretón stressed entertainment rather than instruction in his comic art, his purpose being to afford the audience an enjoyable night in the theater.[18] We may ask, then, what prompted him to moralize so much in *The Phony Education?*

First, his moralizing attitude pertains to an ancient tradition of "books, the corrupters of men." This attitude can be seen in many prominent authors and literary works; for example, St. Jerome, who in the fourth century drastically reduced his references to pagan authors;[19] Chapter VI of *Don Quixote,* where the mad knight's friends burn his romances of chivalry in order to bring him back to reason; and Mariano José de Larra's *El casarse pronto y mal* (1832), which shows a young wife spoiled by French sentimental novels. Bretón's play of 1830 and Larra's article of 1832 carry the same message: an excessively liberal education is not a good thing, especially in women.[20]

Second, Bretón may have sensed moral protest in the air. His *Phony Education* acts as a precursor of the moralizing dramas of the 1860s and 1870s, with their severe *raisonneurs*. The plays of later authors such as Tamayo y Baus and López de Ayala are deeply concerned with nineteenth century materialism (or alleged materialism) and with the effects of wealth, the newspapers, and the modern state on Spanish society.

Third, the moral tone of the play was designed to please Fernandine Spain, for the posture of the Bourbons was very moralistic. But Bretón did not often display the overt righteousness of other nineteenth century authors, either Spanish or, in English literature, Henry Arthur Jones and Arthur Wing Pinero.[21] He viewed the theater primarily as recreation, in the highest sense of this term: it caused delight and provided some instruction.

V   Gilding the Lie (Achaques a los vicios, *1825*)

In *Gilding the Lie,* Don Esteban is given to gambling, which he

The Early Theater: 1824-1833

excuses by saying he has many debts to pay, and in truth he does have many creditors, since his wife Ana spends a fortune on luxuries, while her mother Doña Gerónima wastes another fortune on exquisite parties and viands. Two gamblers fleece Don Esteban at cards, and his servants also cheat him. The one honest person and friend is Don Justo, the *raisonneur,* who periodically stands aside from the main action to explain the moral;[22] he also helps Don Esteban and his wife return to the path of virtue. Finally, the servants are dismissed, the gamblers apprehended, and the selfish, foolish mother-in-law put in her place. Don Esteban will economize and Don Justo will help him.

Much can be learned from *Gilding the Lie* about Bretón and the development of his theater. In Act I, scene viii, the two crooked gamblers, Fermín and Cipriano, give long speeches explaining their past; Bretón quickly abandoned wooden passages of this kind, which do not appear in his later plays. In the same scene there are also many gambling terms (*echarle el tigre, levantando muertos, gurupié*), with an interesting ethical footnote: "These technical terms from the game of Monte, which appear in italics, are well known to cardsharks. Their definitions are omitted here because, besides being prolix, they would hardly edify youth" (*Obras 1850,* I, 50).

VI The Frank and Candid Man (El ingenuo, *1828*)

Don Ramón is the *ingenuo,* the man who always speaks frankly no matter how inopportune the occasion. If he doesn't like someone he tells him so:

DON JORGE: What harshness! You ought
to be less distrustful
of your friends.
DON RAMÓN: Are you
my friend? Since when? (Act I, scene v)

Ramón has been attracted by two girl cousins, Casilda, who is too stern with men, and Teresa,[23] who loves them all. Teresa's father, the old miser Don Zoilo, wants to marry her to a wealthy man without putting up a dowry; naturally, Don Ramón's great fortune interests him.

Two other suitors, Don Jorge and Don Matías, appear on the

scene. The latter is a poetaster who writes colossal and awful melodramas (*comedias disparatadas*), which, within Bretón's play, are a critical reflection on the Madrilenian theater of that period, characterizing "the bulk of theatrical fare of the years 1800 to 1830."[24] Ramón and Jorge fight a duel over Teresa in which Ramón spares his opponent's life after disarming him. He later receives a letter advising him that his principal debtor has lost all his money, but ever the candid man (*el ingenuo*) he lets his own resultant bankruptcy be known. Don Zoilo rejects him now. At the play's end Casilda and Teresa remain unwed and Jorge and Ramón become fast friends.

The Frank and Candid Man (1828) resembles Boutet de Monvel's *L'Amant Bourru,*[25] which Bretón had translated and later staged in 1830, and also his own famous play, *The Country Bumpkin (El pelo de la dehesa,* 1840). In all three plays, the candid lover is the same, and certain concepts are identical, for example, the derogation of the nineteenth century. The nineteenth century is the uncandid age, the century of frauds and deceit (*petardos, maula*); one often encounters this idea in Bretón's theater.[26] But perhaps the greatest value of *The Frank and Candid Man* is the light it throws on censorship, which profoundly affected Bretón and his contemporaries.

CHAPTER 3

Censorship and Several Plays of Bretón

I *Bretón on Censorship*

ON two occasions, at least, Manuel Bretón de los Herreros complained about the effects of censorship on his plays. In his *Arte de la declamación* (1852), he had this to say about the period 1823-1833, the last ten years of the reign of Ferdinand VII, and 1833-1843, the decade of "reestablishment of public liberties," following Ferdinand's death:

Once the impulse was given, there was no holding back, not even for an instant, and since the reestablishment of public liberties coincided with the unlimited liberty of the school known as *Romantic* (also imported from the French, who had taken it from the Germans), dramatic poetry took a marvelous flight in Spain and displayed a feverish activity which threatened to kill it by excess, whereas previously it had died of inanition. Is this to be wondered at, if the stage suddenly threw off the yoke of friarly censorship [*censura frailera*] and also that of the terrible, tyrannical *unities, obstacles to talent and executioners of the imagination?*[1]

The key to the theatrical inanition of the years 1823-1833 is the phrase "the yoke of friarly censorship," which may be construed to mean absolutist censorship. Although Bretón had to write for the censor throughout his entire career (his last work, *Los sentidos corporales* [1867] being approved by the official theater censor, Narciso Serra,)[2] after 1833 the scrutiny of the plays was not friarly; the new censors belonged to a nonabsolutist species.

Bretón's most definitive statement on censorship appears in a footnote he wrote to the 1850 edition of his play *The Frank and Candid Man (El ingenuo),* which was first staged in 1828, five years before the death of Ferdinand VII. The footnote reads:

This play, without doubt the weakest of the collection, was written in a few days, and its plot was not up for discussion at a time when a most rigorous and suspicious censorship weighed heavily on press and theater. To show clearly the disadvantages of excessive veracity, without putting prominent truths in the mouth of the protagonist, which might result in profound consequences, was the same as aborting, so to speak, a comic thought worthy of broader explanation. When developing the character of the *Ingenuo,* the author had to impose upon himself greater prudence than that demanded by the story of the play and the laws of refined society. The character therefore was necessarily incomplete and the lesson ineffective. The *Pleraque et praesens in tempus omittat* of Horace beset him when he formed the ideas of his play and developed them in the dialogue.[3]

Bretón was noted for his comic muse and festive air, which are frequently mentioned by his contemporaries and by later critics of the nineteenth century.[4] A careful examination of *The Frank and Candid Man* in the light of the footnote just cited will show the awesome power of absolutist censorship over Bretón as a comediographer; it will also show the effect censorship has on laughter, which, as George Meredith and Henri Bergson have pointed out, is a social phenomenon.

II *"Friarly Censorship" and* The Frank and Candid Man

The Frank and Candid Man was first staged at the Cruz theater on November 13, 1828, and twenty-two years later Bretón added to it his footnote on censorship. First the note says: "This play, without doubt the weakest of the collection, was written in a few days...." Bretón obviously thought little of *The Frank and Candid Man* and before his death in 1873 he omitted it from his document, "Plan for a New Edition of My Works";[5] to be sure, it did not appear in the large five volume edition of the collected *Obras* in 1883. Nevertheless, the literary critic may take exception to Bretón's judgement. The play is not as bad as he seems to think, and one can only conjecture that when belittling it he had in mind what he might have accomplished had the censor not stayed his hand.

Bretón's note continues "...its plot was not up for discussion at a time when a most rigorous and suspicious censorship weighed heavily on press and theater." The fact of "friarly censorship" is on his mind here, but it is not immediately clear to the reader why it was taken so seriously in connection with *The Frank and Candid*

Man rather than, say, with *Marcela,* one of his most famous plays, which was staged on December 30, 1831, just three years later. On reflection, however, the reader perceives a lifting of the veil.

In Bretón's early theater, nothing of possible public controversy appears — religious, political, or economic; all strife and conflict are reduced to the family, where they center around the marriage of a young man and woman.[6] Humor under the absolutist censorship of 1823-1833 was solely domestic. In the case of *Marcela,* both the plot and humor are naturally associated with the family, since they concern a beautiful young widow who holds three suitors at the end of a string. Censorship is redundant with respect to *Marcela,* merely limiting a domestic comedy to the scope of the family, where it would remain even if there were no coercion. This explains why *Marcela* is the most acceptable of Bretón's early works: he was writing as Bretón and not as Bretón with the censor at his side. *The Frank and Candid Man,* on the other hand, has a broader theme, namely, the effects of indiscreet veracity and misanthropy on the person in whom they reside and upon his victims. Although such a theme may include the family, it need not stop there, but may also encompass prelates, merchants, and ministers of sate; indeed, it is applicable to persons of all stations, and coercion of any kind restricts the artist in his work.

The remainder of Bretón's footnote, from the words "To show clearly the disadvantages of excessive veracity" to the Latin phrase quoted from Horace, contains the heart of the matter, because here Bretón the artist tells in a few choice words how censorship hurt his play; in effect, he explains how it hurts all comic works of art in the theater. Thus it is a universal statement written by a practical man,[7] the artist, which philosophers might consider in their studies on aesthetics. The key phrase is "prominent truths" (*verdades de bulto*).

In Acts I and II of *The Frank and Candid Man,* Don Ramón speaks out bluntly on five occasions to each of five other characters in the play, insulting them with the naked truth (which arises from his "excessive veracity"). His first victim is the avaricious Don Zoilo, who seeks a wealthy husband for his daughter. Flattering Ramón, Don Zoilo's fulsome praise accumulates so many adjectives that it becomes comical:

Usted es noble, juicioso,	You are noble, sagacious,
amable, rico, bizarro,	affable, illustrious, brave,

sensible, gracioso, justo,	compassionate, gentle, just,
comedido, buen cristiano,	prudent, a good Christian,
instruido, complaciente,	learned, kind,
formal, prudente, sensato....	truthful, sensible, wise....
(Act I, scene iii)	

An aposiopesis appears in the text after *sensato,* for Dom Ramón cuts him short. The audience can see, and the reader imagine, the graceless miser caught off balance, on tiptoes and stammering, his beard trembling, with another string of adjectives in his teeth. He is a *fantoche,* a marionette dangling from a string, a figure from the Italian *commedia dell'arte,* and as such is most emphatically funny.

The same kind of humor, which Henri Bergson associates with mechanical rigidity or inelasticity (*raideur mécanique*),[8] takes place when Don Ramón tells his rival, Don Jorge, that they are not kindred spirits ("We don't get along.... Are you my friend? Since when?"). Don Jorge, trying to be nice to Ramón, has been speaking of friendship, but the latter with his bluntness catches him off balance too, and the audience laughs (Act I, scene v).

Ramón's frankness with Teresa in Act I, scene vii, is also comical, as is his artless way in Act II, scene v, where he tells the disdainful — or allegedly disdainful! — Casilda that she does indeed like men.

The last target of Ramón's candor is the poetaster, Don Matías, who shares the comic laurels of the play with the miser, Don Zoilo. Act II, scene vii, of *The Frank and Candid Man* is the quintessence of Moratín's *La comedia nueva.*[9] Don Matías exclaims:

> In my melodrama there are
> supernatural episodes: ruins,
> plagues, shipwrecks, phantoms,
> and many other wonders.
> ....
> and it describes in *redondillas*
> the pyramids of Egypt,
> customs from China,
> the death of Julius Caesar
> and earthquake of Lima.

Don Matías is Folly's own author, her favorite son. He is a risible animal, and so are we, his audience.[10]

It becomes clear now what Bretón meant when he said he wanted

Censorship and Several Plays of Bretón

to place prominent truths (*verdades de bulto*) in Don Ramón's mouth but was unable to do so. In *The Frank and Candid Man* he hoped to show "the disadvantages of excessive veracity," which is a question of meaning and form, or *fondo y forma,* as Hispanists often say. But censorship denied Bretón an adequate *fondo.* In his footnote of protestation, he seems to be saying something like this to the reader, between the lines:

My hands were tied by the censor. I had a good master, Moratín, and also the comedies of Lope, Moreto, Ruiz de Alarcón and others to go by. I had the form, the vessel of the *comedia,* in my grip.[11] Although noted for my festive air, I was no mere merry andrew, as some people seemed to think.[12] I was prepared to write a series of comedies worthy of Molière, and as he taught France in the seventeenth century, so I would teach Spain in the nineteenth. I was on the threshold of a great theater rather than a theater of *merely's:* instead of Don Zoilo being *merely* a greedy father eager to wed his daughter, I might have made him a greedy father and disciple of Jeremy Bentham, who would see the greatest happiness of all in a wealthy son-in-law! Or I might have made him a grimacing *afrancesado* or *exaltado,* or a rigid abolitionist of all taxation (!), or an absent-minded, mock-heroic Carlist, a classical *miles gloriosus:* a study in permanent, quixotic distraction. I might also have shown a disciple of Calomarde lining his pockets in the name of San Fernando and Spain! Don Zoilo was foolish in my play, yes, and very funny, but I might have made him doubly foolish and funny and even more so. How? With some "prominent truths," such as those just mentioned. In 1828, however, these truths would not have passed the censor. Some critics, Larry included,[13] have accused me of repeating the same theme and even the same plot in my plays, but I, Bretón, ask you, what option did an author have in the decade 1823–1833? I later wrote plays of a disputatious nature, e.g., *La redacción de un periódico,* in 1836; *Flaquezas ministeriales,* in 1838; and *El editor responsable,* in 1842; but before the death of Ferdinand in 1833 one did not write plays such as these because: "...its plot was not up for discussion at a time when a most rigorous and suspicious censorship weighed heavily on press and theater."

This same line of reasoning may be applied to the other characters of *The Frank and Candid Man.* Don Ramón, with his exorbitant candor, might have been a radical from the provinces, or, like Bretón, a military man with some terrible truths, comical truths, to utter about the army. Don Jorge, his rival in love, might have played his sociopolitical opposite, or perhaps Don Zoilo's opposite. The redoubtable Casilda, disdainful of men, might have been a classic *mujer brava* constantly and comically repeating some dictum of the reactionaries against a facile and wooden Teresa, the flirt, who might similarly have repeated and echoed the critical dicta of the *philosophes*. Bretón's choices, without censorship, would have been innumerable. Don Matías, the ridiculous poetaster, might have been elevated to another rank, perhaps that of a Comella publishing an outrageous newspaper or broadsheet.

III *"Friarly Censorship" and the Philosophers*

The study of censorship and Bretón's theater throws a dismal light on the history of Spain in the first third of the nineteenth century. It has been said that laughter is a social gesture, an affirmation of shared values.[14] The philosophers also speak of it as a desirable corrective for society. George Meredith, for example, mentions the "vigilant sense of a collective supervision"; then he says, "Sensitiveness to the comic laugh is a step in civilization. To shrink from being an object of it is a step in civilization. We know the degree of refinement in men by the matter they will laugh at, and the ring of the laugh."[15] Meredith's ideas are in keeping with those of Henri Bergson, who remarks: "Consequently the comic expresses an individual or collective imperfection which calls for an immediate corrective. This corrective is laughter, a social gesture that singles out and represses a special kind of absent-mindedness in men and events."[16] Here is the dismal light. If the reader accepts Meredith's opinion, he must admit that the Spaniards of the 1820s often laughed at trivia, which Bretón himself called "bread and circuses."[17] This discloses something about their "degree of refinement" at the time or their "step in civilization." If the reader accepts Bergson's opinion, he will conclude that owing to censorship, the "social gesture" and "corrective" known as laughter was wanting in the Spanish theater between 1823 and 1833. Had Bretón been unfettered, he alone could have provided the corrective, but he was not free, because "a most rigorous and suspicious censorship weighed heavily on press and theater."

Two more statements of Bergson, when applied to Bretón's theater, reveal the nature of censorship:

1. Now step aside, look upon life as a disinterested spectator; many a drama will turn into a comedy.[18]
2. You would hardly appreciate the comic if you felt yourself isolated from others. Laughter appears to stand in need of an echo.[19]

There is a paradox here. On the one hand, "step aside" (isolate yourself) and dramas will turn into comedies; on the other; do not be isolated and both you and others will laugh. The apparent contradiction is resolved if one reasons that stepping aside, or isolation, refers to the author, whereas the nonisolation or social communion refers to the audience.

Censorship, as Bretón knew it before 1833, destroys both halves of the paradox. Under "friarly censorship" a playwright cannot step aside and be by himself, turning dramas into comedy, for everything in life is made a moral issue, incapable of being humorously treated. In the theater, people are allowed to laugh only at domestic incongruities or similar situations, which ordinarily must be contrived by the nonisolated author. Conversely, under absolutist censorship, people cannot band together, form a viable audience, and laugh at an object of common ridicule. All persons are isolated vis-à-vis the censor, so they cannot correct him or the things he cherishes with their mirth; thus censorship destroys society. In his own eyes the censor needs no correction. He is incorrigible.[20]

Bretón was a good comediographer. If his early plays seem at times trivial, as some critics have observed, the defect came honestly and truly from outside his own talent. He was hampered by censorial restraints.[21]

IV *Post-Fernandine Censorship (1833–1843) and Two Plays of Bretón*

To the casual reader, censorship after 1833 might seem as rigorous as censorship before that year. The "Regulations To Be Observed For the Censorship Of Newspapers," of January 4, 1834, seem extremely severe:

the censors will not permit the publication of writings against Religion, the Monarchy, or the Fundamental Laws, nor of those aimed at exciting rebellion, nor those that urge the infringement of some Law or the disobedience of some Authority, nor those that are "licentious and contrary to good customs"; nor those that are injurious to or defamatory of private persons; nor those that injure "foreign Sovereigns and Governments or excite their subjects to rebellion."[22]

To all appearances, these regulations seem absolute. A phrase such as "licentious and contrary to good customs" provides enough breadth to prohibit the printing of anything the censors deem inimical.

That censorship continued to have a rigorous, and ostensibly an absolute, nature may also be seen in the pages of an American traveler, Mr. Severn Treackle Wallis, who wrote in 1853: "The freedom of the press in Spain is guarantied ... by an express provision of the constitution, which ordains that it shall suffer no restrictions but those to be imposed by law...." This constitutional guarantee had been abused, which induced, in 1848, the Minister of the Interior Sartorius to come up with a scheme of reform. Mr. Wallis did not see the scheme, but he was informed: "that it abounded in excellent sentiments, and extended unlimited freedom to all publications in which there might be no discussion of religion or morals, politics, manners, or legislation."[23] This clause apparently goes beyond the "contrary to good customs" clause cited above, for one need not even offend good customs and manners in order to receive official disapprobation, but merely be disposed to discuss them. Furthermore, outside of "religion or morals, politics, manners, or legislation," what else is there? Were Spanish authors to have "unlimited freedom" to discuss nothing?

Perhaps the reality of post-Fernandine censorship, as opposed to the censorship appearing in written law, is best seen in two plays of Manuel Bretón de los Herreros, namely, *La redacción de un periódico* (1836), and *El editor responsable* (1842). The content of these plays shows that censorship changed a great deal in practice after 1833. Since they were staged within the decade following Ferdinand's death (1833–1842), they serve as a good balance for the plays of Bretón's early period (1824–1833).

V The Newspaper, (La redacción de un periódico, *1836*)

The Newspaper continues the Moratinian-Bretonian plot of a young couple opposed to the *senex* figure.[24] Agustín and Amelia want to get married, but her father, the newspaper proprietor, wants her to visit an aging, sick, childless uncle in Santander in order to insure her getting the inheritance. He also plans to marry her to the son of another uncle, a successful merchant. In the end, however, true love is victorious; the designing father is discomfited.

The Newspaper, however, does not keep to the former Bretonian mold, since its author now places several prominent truths (*ver-

dades de bulto) in the mouths of his characters. First of all, the editor, Don Fabricio, envies the economic security of yesteryear:

> Where are you, for I see you not,
> oh kindly era of the
> *Correo literario y mercantil?*[25]
> Without disputes, without rivals,
> its publishers did flourish,
> although it lived a slave
> of friarly censorship.   (Act I, scene i)

Friarly censorship was bad, and the throne may have cast a pall over society, but at least there was financial prosperity for the one or two newspapers allowed to exist in Spain. The new rivals and "plague of publishers" demonstrate for the reader not only an economic struggle for newspaper proprietors but also a relaxation of censorship. Journalism grew because public opinion grew and became variegated; hence the disputes and the fact that "every beardless youth" wanted to take pen in hand. The phrase "it lived a slave of friarly censorship" also indicates that whatever restraints were still in existence in 1836 were nonmonastic, that is to say, nonabsolutist.

Don Fabricio continues his speech, giving an historical account of the years 1833–1836:

> Thus in three calendar years
> at least thirty newspapers perished,
> and all of them built castles in the air
> which soon had vanished.

Once again the play stresses the economic side of the picture; newspaper men were as much concerned about money as news (a preoccupation surely not confined to the 1830s). Fabricio names some twenty-seven papers that failed during the triennium, and his list is unquestionably historical, for twelve of them are listed in the index of a recent *History of Spanish Journalism,* and the other lesser known journals have namesakes from an earlier or later period.[26] With names like *El Boletín de Comercio* and *La Abeja* sounding in the audience's ear, Fabricio's list is quite convincing.

The words of Fabricio, as he reads his list, suggest that ministerial chicanery was a substitute for absolutist censorship:

> The venerable *Correo*
> died of a *coup d'état;*
> ....
>
> The *Aurora* died in eclipse,
> victim of a mandarin;
> ....
>
> The ministerial lightning-bolt
> opened up a veritable pantheon
> for the *Eco de la Opinión,*
> the *Tiempo,* the *Universal*
> and the Cínife,....[27] (Act I, scene i)

This implication of chicanery is in keeping with the plot of *The Newspaper,* in which Don Tadeo[28] is persuaded to publish a pro-ministerial editorial by a promise to enter him on the government's payroll; hitherto he had run antiministerial leaders in the hope of causing sensation and increasing sales. Thus the newspapers themselves were guilty of chicanery, the kind of slyness that did not and could not exist under absolutist censorship.

The Regulations of Censorship of 1834, referred to above, forbade the publication of writings "licentious and contrary to good customs" and also of those that were "injurious and defamatory of private persons." But in Bretón's play, Fabricio says:

> I was referring to that newspaper
> which injures us
> with such unwonted insolence.   (Act I, scene iii)

The "unwonted insolence" of this fictitious newspaper, a mirror of reality, implies that the law of 1834 was being violated. Consequently, the censorship statutes must have been more elastic than they appear at first glance.

At the end of the first act of *The Newspaper,* many subscribers come to the office to cancel their subscriptions, but one man, Antonio Pérez, plans to sign up for a subscription, providing the editors print a certain article denouncing the ministry. Don Tadeo, who is supposed to run a neutral newspaper, agrees to publish it, saying: "Anyhow / I won't profit very much / defending the government" (Act I, scene vi). Since Don Tadeo will support or oppose the government to suit his pocketbook, this passage clearly shows the limited nature of post-Fernandine censorship as it appears in Bretón's theater; one cannot imagine one of Ferdinand VII's friarly censors countenancing the whimsical support of a government. This passage also shows the roguish nature of the newspaper business.[29]

In the second act of *The Newspaper,* one perceives that the *verdades de bulto* ("prominent truths": the vicissitudes of the newspaper world) lead to broader comedy and *costumbrismo.* An actress comes to the editorial room to complain about the theater reviewer, who has called her "old," an interdicted word for the ladies; in the ensuing argument, the words *adulta* and *adúltera* and *silva* and *silba* ("adult," "adultress"; and "Silva," "hiss") are most unhappily confused. When Agustín flatters the actress in order to appease her, his beloved Paula begins to question his fidelity. A fierce captain of *guerrilleros* comes to challenge the editor to a duel. Fabricio is frantically translating articles from the French, to fill out a column, and one imagines him surrounded by ever-mounting tons of foolscap, but there is still insufficient material for this illustrious journal. A poet submits some detestable verses, and the demanding printers' foreman comes to pick up the copy for print. All these scenes lend a fullness to *The Newspaper* that is completely wanting in earlier plays such as *The Frank and Candid Man:* there is even reference to the Carlist war in the north.

The whole second act, moreover, is a *cuadro de costumbres* within which the dramatic family conflict of Paula and Agustín with her father continues. And one learns something explicit about the daily edition of a newspaper:

> AGUSTÍN: Is there still a lot to go for tonight's edition?
> FOREMAN: It's still in diapers,
>   you might say....
> AGUSTÍN: As usual. No matter:
>   tonight's *Gaceta* will provide us
>   with enough for two columns;
>   later the censors will send back
>   more material; with this
>   and with the session of Parliament,
>   the Stock Market and spectacles,
>   there's more than enough.... (Act II, scene v)

With the materials just mentioned, and with the hastily translated *ripios* (padding) of Fabricio from the French, Agustín will publish the distinguished and illustrious newspaper of Don Tadeo.

Later in Act II, Don Tadeo so speaks of censorship that the reader can clearly see room for a variety of opinions before the government, including opposition:

> He has given me a superb article,
> and his friend two of them ... Ha, ha!
> In opposition, of course:
> we've had enough leniency.
> I have sent them to the censor
> for examination instead of
> those worthless papers
> which bring neither honor nor bread. (Act II, scene ix)

The "worthless papers" (*papeles mojados*) bringing neither honor nor bread are the impartial articles written by Agustín and his colleagues, who seek to publish the truth; but Don Tadeo is interested only in bread — money — and is willing to engage in histrionic opposition to win it.

With respect to censorship, *The Newspaper* presents the critic with two realities: (1) the reality of the playwright himself, which is the flesh-and-blood reality of the reader, and (2) the reality of the characters in the play, Fabricio, Agustín, Don Tadeo, and others, which is the reality of Don Quixote and Sancho as they insist on a true history. Within the reality of Bretón's world, *The Newspaper* passed censorship in 1836 in spite of its indicating that both the government and its official censors are venal and temporizing; no similar work would have passed the friarly censorship prior to 1833. Within the reality of the play, Don Fabricio and the other characters act as if the censorship of 1836 were qualified rather than absolute. I construe their attitude to be a true history, a faithful mirror of the days.

VI The Editor Responsible (El editor responsable, *1842*)

Censorship assumes responsibility or accountability. If the ordinances of the censor are broken, some person or corporation must be held accountable so the censor can exercise sanctions against him, usually in the form of a fine or prison sentence. Some of these sanctions can be seen in *The Newspaper,* where fines are mentioned on several occasions, for example:

FABRICIO:	And has it been censored?
TADEO:	No.
FABRICIO:	Well then, how can it be printed?
TADEO:	It doesn't matter.
AGUSTÍN:	If they denounce it to the civil governor, the fine .... (Act I, scene vi; see also Act V, scene xiv)

In Spain, from 1834 to 1868, a person known as "the editor responsible" was added to the staff of each newspaper; responsibility, that is, legal accountability, was his only reason for existence. Others might write or edit an article, perhaps inflammatory in tone, but he was the one who signed each number of the newspaper, and if the case went to court, it was he who stood in the dock and had to answer all charges. Since his accountability might be reckoned as a two year sentence in jail, the office of editor responsible was an extremely risky one. This legal personage might better have been called "The Scapegoat Editor," and Prime Minister Cánovas had this to say of him and his breed: "for a price they lived [a new kind of slavery] beneath the weight of an endless series of sentences for transgressions they had neither committed nor were able to commit...."[30] As in all risky jobs, there were always openings for new editors responsible, and the pay was high, which attracted young men who might otherwise be unemployed. This well-defined *verdad de bulto* is the basis of Bretón's play of 1842.

The plot of *The Editor Responsible* resembles that of *Die And You Will See,* which had appeared in 1837.[31] In the former play, Josefina, a coquette, and Ana, a stable young lady, work together as seamstresses. Josefina has both Gaspar and Dupré on a string, whereas Ana loves only Gaspar. Dupré writes an inflammatory article against the government for *El Terremoto,* but it is Gaspar, the editor responsible, who may have to do a two year stint in jail for this action. At the end of Act I, the fickle Josefina forsakes Gaspar for Dupré (Gaspar is dead to the world, so to speak, like Pablo in *Die And You Will See*). Dupré has used Romantic language! He has threatened dramatic assassination and suicide! He has conquered her!

Once again, this comedy displays a far greater wealth of ideas, customs, and humor than the plays of 1824–1833. The day of Gaspar's trial, the scene in the waiting chamber of the courtroom, where the crowd makes fun of the *portero,* is one of the most comical Bretón ever penned:

DOORMAN:	I am strict with everybody, but with her ... the poor little girl! So pretty! ... *Homo sum!* A doorman's job does not preclude courtesy. [No quita lo cortés a lo portero.]
3RD CITIZEN:	Did you all hear? *Homo sum!*
1ST CITIZEN:	Since he affirms it, I'll believe it, but I was doubtful ....
3RD CITIZEN:	What?
1ST CITIZEN:	Whether he was a man or a tunafish.
DOORMAN:	Casting doubt on my species! I swear.... But let's keep the peace.
2ND CITIZEN:	Leave him alone....
DOORMAN:	Or I'm apt to....
2ND CITIZEN:	And let's talk about *El Terremoto.* (Act II, scene xi)

With the mention of the inflammatory newspaper, *El Terremoto,* the play returns naturally and gracefully to its prominent truth (*verdad de bulto*): will an innocent young man, an editor responsible, be sentenced to prison for the indiscretion of others? This graceful turning from humor to a weighty truth and back again to humor did not appear in Bretón's early theater, which was bound by absolutist censorship.

One will not forget the love scene of Gaspar and Ana (Act II, scene xvii), or Gaspar's soliloquy right after it:

¿Qúe pena será la suya, ¡señor! por más que discurro....	What can be her affliction? Lord! no matter how much I try to fathom it ....
¿Envidia de su maestra? No. — ¿Amor? Ya he dado en el punto.	Is she jealous of her teacher? No. — Love? Now I've hit the nail on the head.
Anita está gravemente enamorada ... de alguno. Pero este alguno ¿quién es? No lo alcanza mi discurso.	Anita is deeply in love ... with someone. But this someone, who is he? I can't fathom it out.

Censorship and Several Plays of Bretón

A nadie he visto rondarla,
seguirla ... Sólo columbro,

según llora y se compunge,
que debe de ser muy duro
de corazón el objeto
del cariño que barrunto.
Y en verdad que el individuo
en quien sus ojuelos puso
una muchacha tan linda
y no la dice soy tuyo,
vive el cielo que es de piedra,
o tiene estragado el gusto.
Quisiera yo conocer
al Ganimedes oculto
para tener el gustazo
de decirle que es un bruto. —
Pero .., si bien reflexiono ..,
la sensación que produjo
en su pecho la noticia
de mi casamiento; el sumo
interés con que ha mirado
el inminente infortunio
de que acabo de librarme
por milagro; tantos pujos
de llorar cuando me mira;
y callar cuando pregunto
la causa de su dolor,
o responder con singultos....
Me atrevería a apostar,
y no sería un absurdo,
a que yo soy el narciso
de cuyo desdén injusto
se lamenta. Sí, yo soy
el que acelera su pulso;
yo soy el galán incógnito;
yo soy la piedra ... y el bruto!
(Act II, scene xviii)

I've seen no one courting her.
or following her .... I can
    only gather,
since she cries and carries on so,
that the object of her affection
must be very
hard of heart.
And to tell the truth, the man
on whom such a pretty girl
set those little eyes,
if he doesn't tell her I'm yours,
by heaven he's made of stone,
or is depraved in his senses.
I'd like to meet
this hidden Ganimede
and have the great big pleasure
of telling him he's a brute. —
But .., if I think back some ..,
the sensation caused in her breast
by the news of my forthcoming
marriage; the extreme
interest she showed
over my imminent misfortune,
which by a miracle I have just
escaped; such uncontrollable
crying when she looks at me;
and her growing silent when I ask her
the cause of her sorrow,
or answering me with sobs....
I would boldly bet,
and it wouldn't be absurd,
that I am the Narcissus
whose unjust disdain
she grieves over. Yes, I am
the one who quickens her pulse;
I am the unknown loved one;
I am the stone ... and the brute!

Later in the play, a colonel comes to challenge the editor responsible to a duel: dueling is another facet of this comedy's "prominent truth." At the end, after Gaspar's acquittal of the charges against him, the government buys off Dupré with a five thousand franc bribe.[32] True love wins out. Gaspar will marry his beautiful and faithful Anita.[33]

VII A Conclusion Concerning Censorship

Manuel Bretón de los Herreros complained occasionally about the effects of absolutist censorship (*censura frailera*) on the Spanish theater and on his own theater in particular. Such censorship causes inanition. A playwright cannot include prominent truths (*verdades de bulto*) in his plays, with their transcendental consequences, and as a result "his characters are incomplete and his lessons inefficacious." A given author, Bretón himself for example, may understand the censorial mold and produce a somewhat entertaining, light-hearted theater, but the hand of the censor weighs on everything, affecting not only the content of the play but also its mode of expression. Bretón's own plays stand in proof of this statement, for after the diminishing of censorship in 1833 and 1834 they became broader comedy: their humor became more diverse, their customs or manners more widespread, and their love poems more memorable.

Absolutist censorship hampers the liberty of both the private citizen and society. A playwright cannot isolate himself and freely ponder the shortcomings of his country, thereby converting apparently dramatic events into comedy, because the censor, himself a dramatist of sorts, views everything with solemnity. National events are his drama and scarcely a subject for the comic muse. On the other hand, a spectator cannot unite himself to other spectators and form a risible society mocking common faults, because the censor will not brook such laughter, the most telling of all corrections.

The absolutist censor represents perfection[34] and consequently is incorrigible; as the custodian of religion, politics, and economics, he cannot permit the existence of a *comedia corregidora* (a correcting comedy). Since the end of comedy is the correction of two parties, the old and the vicious,[35] the censor will permit only a kind of half-comedy. Thus in Fernandine Spain, Bretón could correct only the old members of a family, the *senex* figures of ancient comedy, and having to do this over and over again he left himself open to the charge of superficiality. Two of Bretón's post-Fernandine plays about the newspaper world clearly show that this alleged weakness on his part is founded on censorial constraints rather than lack of native imagination or talent. His later plays are good comedies, deserving a more reflective criticism than they have generally received. Bretón, the most capable Spanish playwright of the nineteenth century, possessed the art of gracefully turning from humor to prominent truths and back to humor again. His love stories are delightful, and in portraying the society of three decades, he is Spain's Balzac.[36]

CHAPTER 4

The Academy Speech and a Few Plays in Prose

IN the spring of 1837, the Marqués de Molíns and his associates decided to propose Bretón for membership in Spain's Royal Academy of Language. Entrance into the Academy entailed the apparently immodest act of a candidate's presenting his own petition, based on past merits, but the Spaniards of the day had a subterfuge for evading this unseemly custom. Molíns prepared the petition, which Bretón signed, probably without reading it, and then his friend presented it to the Academy on June 1, 1837.[1] Bretón's entrance into the learned society was a model of expedition. The academicians voted for him unanimously on June 8, 1837, and he read his acceptance speech one week later, on June 15, 1837: the entire process had taken two weeks. Shortly before Bretón was admitted to the Academy, he visited the famous teacher, Alberto Lista, who had placed Bretón's portrait on a wall with the words of Ovid written beneath it: "Whatever he attempted to say, was in verse." Inspired perhaps by this incident, Bretón made this motto the subject of his address. He would speak to his new colleagues on the language of the theater; he was to conclude that verse is preferable to prose; of all the verse forms, the most suitable are *romances* and *redondillas*.[2]

I   *The Academy Speech*

Bretón's argument falls into four basic parts, the last of which is most important, since it defines the *comedia* in general, and specifically, the *comedia bretoniana*. First, Bretón believes that "plays should be written in verse" for reasons of tradition and authority. Lope, Calderón, and the other great playwrights wrote in verse, and even Cervantes did so when writing for the theater. There are two noteworthy exceptions, the prose dialogues of Lope de Rueda and the two famous plays of Moratín. Bretón venerates both authors, but their example, no matter how great, will not prevail against the practice of three centuries. Verse, which brings movement and fluency to the theater, is preferable by tradition.

The second part of Bretón's argument is based on the premise that art embellishes reality without disfiguring it. Playing his own devil's advocate, he poses an objection based on verisimilitude. People do not speak in verse, so how can the theater, which copies life, employ it? Bretón replies that playwrights must abandon a perfect imitation. A German actor of humble origin, for example, will play the role of a Spanish king; the plot of a play being staged at night may take place during the day; the stage decorations do not conform exactly to the buildings and scenes around us: similarly, the language of the stage will not be the same as that of everyday life, no, not even when it is written in prose. Bretón's reasoning boils down to this: "Talent and good taste can find means of embellishing truth itself without disfiguring it; whoever does not succeed in doing this is not a poet."

The third part of Bretón's argument is an extension of the first. He writes: "The ear of the audience, and especially of a Spanish audience, very quickly and willingly gets accustomed to the charm of versification, and when the rhyme conforms smoothly to the author's thoughts, the illusion becomes complete. As long as the curtain is raised, one should not think, nor should one even imagine that men can speak in any other fashion."

Bretón goes on to say that dramatic art need not exclude the elegance or magnificence of diction and images found in other poetic compositions, e.g., the sonnet. Nevertheless, the poetry of the *comedia* is generally a rather quick dialogue of questions and answers, give and take, opinions and counteropinions, what one man says, and another, and then another. This does not preclude an occasional long speech, but speeches of more than fifteen or twenty lines are comparatively rare in Bretón, and most of them are far shorter than that. Soliloquies are also comparatively rare, and when they occur they are short. (One might add that in his articles for the *Correo Literario y Mercantil,* Bretón denounces the use of asides in the theater on grounds of inverisimilitude; however, he himself uses them quite often in his plays, and they are quick, brief, rapid, sometimes being a repartee. They make for a dialogue having *fluidez* (fluidity) if not complete *naturalidad* (naturalness):

they are naturalness's embellishment.) Verses in comedy should run smoothly and quickly.

For the literary critic, the fourth part of Bretón's argument is the most important passage on the theory of drama he ever penned, since he distinguishes here between comedy and the more pretentious plays generally called dramas. An imposing drama, he says, one in which high political interests are at stake or in which vehement passions and fierce combat between virtue and crime appear, can get by without the support of verse. But the plays properly called *Comedias* need versification:

A drama whose spectacle is impressive and magnificent, one in which high political interests are stirred up or in which vehement passions are put into play as well as a fierce struggle between virtue and crime, such a drama can sustain itself without the aid of verse, because the story contains other attractions, although none so powerful as verse. But the piece properly called a *comedy,* that is to say, the play whose object is to attack, with the weapons of refined and animated satire, certain social vices which are not precisely crimes; the play which portrays the characters and customs we see every day in the circle of our friends and acquaintances; such a play cannot set its sights so high; it must be very simple in its form, and it must try to capture the good will of its spectators by a live, witty dialogue and harmonious language rather than by some clamorous, imposing action. Without the prestige of history, without the machinery of stage effects, without the pomp of a huge diversified company of actors, the comic poet is left to himself. He needs to bring forth all the forces of his imagination relevant to the end he desires.

From this passage one might construct the definition of a typical Bretonian play: A comedy of everyday characters and customs, of relatively uncomplicated form, with an animated witty dialogue. Written in verse to provide harmony and unity, it is designed to satirize the social vices.

Finally, Bretón takes up the question of which kind of verse is preferable in the *comedia.* Some say octosyllabic verses, especially the *romance,* because they are the least removed from prose. But he himself holds that all kinds of verse are acceptable, depending on their suitability to the scene: "Nor do I propose to set any rules; let this remain free for the study and the poetic instinct of each author." The *romance* and *redondilla* are, generally speaking, the best verses of all, and he is partial to the *redondilla*. He then gives three long examples of *redondillas* from Alarcón, Moreto and Montalbán.

The Academy Speech and a Few Plays in Prose 53

One might compare Bretón's Academy speech with Lope de Vega's *New Art of Writing Comedies* (1609). Both men refuse to prescribe a hard and fast set of rules; both men ask for variety, the source of beauty; and both indicate that they wrote spontaneously, for a large public. Both men also dominated the theater of their day. The principal difference between these two authors appears to be lyrical rather than dramatic. Lope's songs and lyrical poetry alone would give him a high place in Spanish literature, whereas Bretón's lyrical poetry, which fills volume V of *Obras 1883,* would make him an interesting but minor poet of the nineteenth century. Lope's lyrical prowess permeates his theater; Bretón's plays become truly lyrical only from time to time.

II Five Comedies In Prose

Bretón practiced what he preached in his Academy speech throughout his entire theatrical career. He wrote some sixty-four full length comedies and dramas, almost all of them in verse, nevertheless, in spite of his preference for verse, he turned to prose in five comedies. Two of these are early: *The Young Old Codger (A la vejez viruelas,* 1817) and *Gilding the Lie (Achaques a los vicios,* 1825). Three are of later composition: *Independence (La independencia,* 1844), *Birds of a Feather (La cabra tira al monte,* 1853), and *The Girl at the Counter (La niña del mostrador,* 1854). Why, we may ask, did he, so obviously committed to the versification of plays, write these five in prose? Can we learn anything from them? The answer to this question for the early plays listed above will be different from the answer for the later ones. In a footnote to the 1850 edition of *The Young Old Codger,* Bretón tells us explicitly why he wrote it in prose. As a budding playwright he had come under the influence of Moratín:

he [Bretón] had the good fortune of getting hold of the works of Moratín, whom he had only known superficially until then, and possessed of an almost superstitious attachment to this great author, it seemed to him that, since Moratín's two best productions ... were written in prose, no author, and much less a beginner, should dare to use any other language in his own works. He [Bretón] soon gave up this idea, but he never gave up admiring the immortal *Inarco.*

The influence of Moratín, the immortal *Inarco,* was very great, and the young Bretón paid him tribute by writing two of his early plays in prose. However, one must still account for the prose plays of 1844, 1853, and 1854, which were written long after Bretón had outgrown his "almost superstitious attachment" to Moratín.

III Independence (La Independencia, *1844*)

Independence has three plots. The first is the independence of the bachelor, Don Agustín, which is overcome by his growing love for Isabel. A rival for Isabel appears in the person of his malicious housekeeper, Nicanora, and an apparent rival in a beautiful neighbor, Doña Amparo. The second plot concerns the identity of the foundling child and the love of Amparo for the captain, Don Juan. The third plot touches on the events leading up to March 1820 and the political revolt of Riego. Of these, only the first plot is characteristic of a Bretonian comedy and should, according to Bretón, go into verse. The other two plots, which gradually take over the play, are more like what Bretón described in his Academy speech as "A drama whose spectacle is impressive and magnificent, one in which high political interests are stirred up...." Indeed, the treachery of Nicanora and her nephew Jesualdo lead to "vehement passions and fierce struggle," and thus, "...such a drama can sustain itself without the aid of verse."

In other words, *Independence* is a hybrid play with strong leanings toward a drama of impressive spectacle. Consequently, Bretón wrote it in prose.

IV Birds of a Feather (La cabra tira al monte, *1853*)

Fernando and Eugenia, two young lovers, are frustrated by the arrogance of her ne'er-do-well father, who lives beyond his means. As a result of the father's misdeeds, Fernando substitutes for another man in the military lottery and goes off to the wars (the play takes place in 1834, during the Carlist civil war.) Five years pass, and the separation of the lovers seems irremediable. The selfish father still uses his daughter for his own ends and will have her marry the worthless son of worthless social climbers for their money. But by chance Fernando, now a colonel, is lodged under the military statues of the day in the house of Eugenia's future in-laws. Love wins out, and the worthless father and social climbers have an unverisimilar change of heart.

Concerning Bretón's use of prose in *Birds of a Feather*, one might argue that the first act, which typifies a Bretonian comedy, should have been written in verse. But the last two acts are meant to be "a drama whose spectacle is impressive and magnificent," the kind of theater that can be cast in prose. And now a pattern is discerned. Bretón's prose plays are transitional; they are paving the way for the so-called "high comedy" (*alta comedia*) of Manuel Tamayo y Baus. Some of Tamayo's early plays were written in verse (*Joan of Arc,* 1847; *Virginia,* 1853; *The Lady Magnate,* 1854; *The Snowball,* 1856); but after 1856, down to his last play in 1870, a total of seven plays, Tamayo wrote everything in prose. These later plays, offspring of Bretón's *Birds of a Feather,* were noted for their sudden conversions, happy endings, dramatic changes of heart, "vehement passions and fierce struggle between virtue and crime." They could, at least in theory, "sustain themselves without the aid of verse."

V The Girl at the Counter (*La niña del mostrador, 1854*)

Here, the same pattern appears. The first part of the play (Act I, or Acts I and II) are Bretonian: a young boy and a young girl fall in love, but an obstacle presents itself in the form of an avaricious father. Act III ceases to be Bretonian comedy and becomes "high comedy" or "Tamayesque." Everything appears, so to speak, in capital letters. Virtue confronts Vice. Youth confronts Age. The Orphan finds Salvation. The Sinner finds Repentance. The name of God appears. There is a Sudden Conversion, a Deus Ex Machina, and a Happy Ending. There is cathartic anagnorisis: the Bad Man turns out to be the Orphan's Father and immediately becomes Good. This quick change of form at the end of the *alta comedia* is not lyrical or comic; it is prosaic, and in the eyes of those who lived at the time (the 1850s and 1860s), dramatic. An example of this prosaic quality is the extremely strong use of epithets: bondad *inmensa,* pasión *bastarda,* vicio más *ruin, sórdida* avaricia.

Between 1844 and 1854 Bretón wrote twenty-three plays (sixteen full-length plays, and seven of one act). Three of these plays, *Independence, Birds of a Feather,* and *The Girl at the Counter,* differ from the others. They are more like "an impressive and magnificent drama" than a Bretonian comedy; they expose, rather than dramatize, a most complicated plot; and they resemble the works of Tamayo y Baus in the 1860s, the *alta comedia.* Hence they were written in prose.[3]

CHAPTER 5

Marcela *and Her Twin Sisters*

I   *The Simplicity of* Marcela

THE reader of *Marcela* is immediately struck by the play's simplicity. The young widow Marcela has three suitors from whom she is to choose a spouse. The three men appear in the first act, present their cases in the second act, and are judged by Marcela in the third act in her own court of love (scenes xi–xiii). All are found wanting for some reason, and she will marry none of them. Until someone conquers her heart, she will cherish her widow's independence.

Because of the plot's simplicity, two things stand out in the play: (1) the characters, who reflect the customs of the time, and (2) the author's versification. The most unforgettable character of *Marcela* is the dandy,[1] Don Agapito Cabriola y Bizcochea, whose name suggests a fondness for pastries and dancing. He so resembles a figure from the *commedia dell'arte* that the other characters twice call him a puppet and Harlequin; he is also referred to as a *muñeco, bicho, chinche, mono,* and *orangután.* He is the model of nineteenth century dandyism, or *lechuguinismo*. The reader interested in dandyism might study the etching in Fernando Díaz-Plaja's *La vida española en el siglo XIX*. The young man depicted there, "El Perfecto Currutaco," might have been Bretón's own Don Agapito; one need only place a paper cone in his hand, filled with caramels and sweetmeats, to rename the etching "Don Agapito Cabriola y Bizcochea."

Another memorable character is a *Weltschmerz* poet of the 1830s, Amadeo Tristán del Valle (a name implying love, sadness, and a valley of tears). The beautiful widow has inspired his sudden love, which he expresses in a gloomy sonnet; he signs his name to the sonnet with a flourish, and when Marcela rejects his suit, offering him friendship instead, he leaves the stage for the final time reciting his heartfelt *silvas:*

> No, no, be my enemy,
> for the miserable Amadeus is not worthy
> before holy altars at your side to take to himself
> the placid crown of Hymen.
> Meanwhile my woes,
> far from you, weeping, on the shores
> of Manzanares' lentitude,
> I with doeful voice
> will offer to the wind sad songs.
> Adieu! (Act III, scene xii)

Shortly afterward he adds some verses referring to himself as "the new Macías," the great lover, who dies a victim of Marcela's cruelty.

In another person's mouth Amadeo's *silvas* might convey strong emotion, but knowing his histrionics, we look for overstatement and find it, especially in "Manzanares' lentitude." Various rivers in Spain symbolize different ideas; e.g., the Tagus, the royal river, the river of Garcilaso de la Vega, represents dignity and poetry as well as Spain itself; the Guadiana, which runs underground a long distance, stands for whatever is secret or hidden; and the Manzanares, the insignificant river of Madrid, is the butt of jokes, the exact opposite of the Tagus. Any mention of its dignity or grandeur is made ironically, and so Amadeo's promise to weep on the banks of the slow Manzanares becomes comical. Bretón is making fun of Romantic lugubriousness.[2] He also parodies Romantic exuberance when the captain describes what a published work by Amadeo would be like:

> If it isn't some frightful
> novel with specters,
> and violence and dungeons,
> and souls in purgatory and suicides...
> and, in brief, everything now in vogue. (act I, scene viii)

The third and most eligible suitor, Captain of Artillery Martín Campana y Centellas, brings Marcela both the virtues and the shortcomings of an army man. Generous and straightforward, he is also extremely brusque. His love proposals sound like the preparations for a military campaign, in which a soldier scouts the terrain and considers all avenues of approach. He cites the pros and cons of contracting marriage and offers himself as a solution to the young woman's dilemma. Marcela, remembering her unhappy marriage, rejects this immature man.

Contrary to a prevalent opinion, Marcela is not an incorrigible coquette. Secure in her youth, beauty, wealth, and widowhood, she is lighthearted, but does not attract suitors out of vanity, merely to play with them. Naturally attractive to men, she is also being goaded into marriage by her uncle, Don Timoteo, a ceaseless talker who says everything twice, by way of synonyms. Her advice to Agapito on avoiding effeminacy and to the narcissistic Amadeo is sound. Most significant is her attitude toward widowhood, a source of independence for young women in Spain:

Sensible soy como toda,	Like all women I am sensitive,
no me pienso emparedar,	I don't want to wall myself in,
pero me pongo a temblar,	but I begin to tremble
con sólo hablarme de bodas.	at the mere thought of marriage.
me hallo bien con mi reposo,	I am happy in my repose,
con mi dulce libertad,	in my sweet liberty,
y temo hallar en verdad	and I truly fear I'll find
un tirano en un esposo.	a tyrant in a spouse.
Mas si al fin, como mujer,	But if at last, as a woman,
me es forzoso sucumbir,	I find I must succumb,
ya que yo lo he de sufrir,	seeing I must put up with him,
yo me lo quiero escoger.	I want to choose him myself.

(Act III, scene ii)

The outstanding critic, Le Gentil, refers to Don Martín Campana y Centellas, the captain, as "l'un des fantoches de *Marcela*." If he is indeed a *fantoccio* (a marionette), and Agapito a Harlequin or puppet, as he is called by other characters in the play, then the awkward poet, Amadeo, and the pleonastic abuser of synonyms, Don Timoteo, might also be considered puppets. They are rigid in their demeanor. It might be fruitful for some director to cast the play in this light: Timoteo as Pantaloon, Agapito as Harlequin, the captain as a *miles gloriosus,* and Amadeo as a Doctor-poet.[3]

II *The Versification of* Marcela

In a footnote to the 1850 edition of *Marcela,* Bretón tells us how

Marcela and Her Twin Sisters

this comedy marks the beginning of those plays properly called Bretonian. Prior to its premiere on December 30, 1831, he had adhered to Neoclassical rules, but now he was to shed them. The change did not take place all at once, for *Marcela* is a model of unity; the action occurs in one room of the young widow's house before and after a midday meal, and the six characters focus their thoughts on one sole problem: which of the three suitors will Marcela marry? (*which of the three* is the subtitle: *Marcela ¿A cuál de los tres?*). The play, however, definitely breaks with some rules of the past, and Bretón will continue this rupture throughout the 1830s.

Bretón's footnote to the 1850 edition of *Marcela* has this to say:

With this play the author opened a new and freer route to his imagination. For previous plays he had dared to use no other meter than the octosyllabic *romance,* because it was recommended by very respectable authorities, and also because it is best adapted to the liveliness and nature of dialogue. All the while, the author felt a terrible urging to use consonantal rhyme, he was burning with desire to let his pen, far too disciplined, romp a little in the field of poetry. Studying time and again Lope, Calderón, Tirso, Rojas, Moreto, and Alarcón, he envied them their happy independence in this area, which was so fertile in beautiful creations. All contemporary poets (those of 1830) were loosening and some were even beginning to shake off entirely the academic yoke. Constant in his literary faith, though indeed not the blind sectarian of an exclusive school, the author managed to preserve himself from the pitiful aberrations others fell into. But he had to be honest with himself and test his powers to see if it were not possible to reconcile the vigorous portrayal of feelings and characters, the *vis cómica* of dialogue, and the naturalness of language with a more diverse, artificial, and ornate versification, not to the extent however that it would be too lyrical and too picturesque. As he kept progressing in this experiment, he noticed that for dialogued verses in the theater, the consonantal rhyme served him as well as when he used it in other small poems of a different genre. Moreover, far from being an obstacle to each character's speaking the way he should in a given situation, consonantal rhyme helped the author formulate his thoughts in a more concise and witty way; it suggested other new thoughts to him, it stimulated and fired his imagination, and at every moment it demonstrated to him the truth in the idea of *rima inspiratrice.* The extraordinary triumph of *Marcela* was due in large part if not entirely to the new vogue; the author, who was using consonantal rhyme in an effort to please the public, decided never to abandon it in the future.[4]

This passage shows that the Romanticism of the 1820s and 1830s was causing poets to cast off "the academic yoke" that had bound them to the rules of Neoclassicism. Some poets fell into "pitiful aberrations," that is, Wertherian suicidal love, *Weltschmerz* narcissism, Romantic exuberance ("specters, violence, dungeons, souls in purgatory"), and also excessive language, e.g., *esdrújulos*.[5] But Bretón took a middle ground in *Marcela*. Breaking with the past, he nevertheless accepted much of its substance. *Marcela* is a simple unified play, as much so in its plot and scenes as Moratín's *El sí de las niñas,* but in its use of verse it departs radically from Moratín. *Marcela* makes free use of *redondillas, romances,* and *quintillas,* and also adds a *letrilla,* a sonnet, *silvas, décimas,* and prose for two letters.

Bretón's new use of rhyme deserves further comment. *Marcela* opens with a scene in *redondillas* in which the effeminate Agapito is doing embroidery while Marcela weaves a leather case. Don Timoteo and Juliana are also present. These verses are in keeping with the liveliness of the action, where the "synonymiferous" Timoteo clashes with the spirited Juliana, and Agapito is an obvious figure of fun.

In scene iii, Juliana delivers a long soliloquy of assonant lines in *ú* ("un romance agudo en *ú*"),[6] supposedly directed to a servant girl next door. In addition to words like *sur, gandul, aún, tú, juventud,* Bretón is forced to employ other languages, expletives, unusual names, place names, and even a letter of the alphabet to maintain his rhyme: such words are *canezú, Galluz, Pedro Eguiluz, Q* [*cue*], *¿prum!, non plus, piú, padetú*. In Spanish, these seventy-six assonant verses in *ú* are an extraordinary feat, contrasting with the more facile *redondillas* and *quintillas* before and after them. A source of wonderment for the audience, they are not mere verbal padding (*ripios*), since Juliana here sums up the plot of the comedy, the courting of Marcela by three suitors. The affected use of words from French, Latin, and Italian also conforms to the character of Agapito, whom she describes. And the captain of artillery has a mouth like a howitzer (*obús*)!

One may similarly account for the other verse forms, down to the *décimas* at the end, where Marcela recites forty lines explaining the state of women in Spain:

>A girl desires a wedding
>to enjoy her liberty,
>and in her spouse awaits her

> greater captivity.
> In every state and sphere
> a woman is unhappy;
> she is only less unfortunate
> as a widow free,
> without husband or relative
> to whom she lives in chains. (Act III, scene xiii)

Marcela's words reveal the meaning of Bretón's play. He is not engaged in drollery for the sake of drollery. He depicts several characters and customs of 1830 Spain, the most prominent of which is the social position of women.[7] Above all, he has captured for us the special role of the young widow.

Bretón spoke before of *rima inspiratrice,* of form's inspiring content. His new, freer use of rhyme seems to have inspired a new kind of play, for Marcela does not marry any one of the three suitors, as she might have in his earlier theater.[8]

III Marcela's *Twin Sisters*

In 1834 Mariano José de Larra, having observed a pattern in Bretón's plays, wrote these words in his review of the latter's *A Sweetheart for the Girl: (Un novio para la niña)* "This poet has given us three consecutive plays in which, although repeating himself, he has succeeded in fashioning three different comedies. A simple and virtuous young girl and three suitors [serve] for the plot of all of them. Another author would have been hard-pressed to make just one play out of that, but the author of *A Sweetheart for the Girl* has come up with three different dramas."[9] Molíns, writing in 1883, adds to Larra's argument and calls Chapter XII of his biography of Bretón "The Twin Sisters of Marcela, 1830 to 1835." The "twin sisters" to *Marcela* (1831) are *Love's Referee (Un tercero en discordia,* 1833), *A Sweetheart for the Girl (Un novio para la niña,* 1834), *This World a Farce (Todo es farsa en este mundo,* 1835), and *Her Fateful Moment (Un cuarto de hora,* 1842).

Love's Referee is a *carrusel amatorio,*[10] an amorous merry-go-round in which Luciana, the girl with the beautiful eyes (Act I, scene v), asks for a referee to help her choose between her two suitors. The referee chooses ... himself! This comedy contains many of the phenomena that had appeared in Bretón's previous plays: e.g., a poetaster criticizing Moratín, a burlesque threat of Romantic suicide (Act III, scene iv), a free use of proverbs, references to literature (e.g., *The Adventures of Gil Blas*), and a parody of Calderonian verses (Act II, scene i). It also contains some scenes showing why Bretón is generally described as a comediographer of manners and customs; Le Gentil even refers to him as the Balzac of Spain, the man one must read if he is to know the Spanish middle class of the early nineteenth century.[11] In Nemesia, the old servant of a Spanish widower, the reader sees the real boss of a household, who tells her master when to come and go. Some speeches of Don Rodrigo (the referee) give a thorough description of Spanish eating habits (e.g., Act I, scene ii) and of the Prado (Act II, scene ii).[12] There are also references to the *ambigú* (buffet supper), the *café* and *tertulia* (social gathering).

Two passages from *Love's Referee* are exceptionally funny. Don Ciriaco, the old widower and father of Luciana, is accustomed to speak with his hands, and as he addresses Don Rodrigo, he strips each and every button off his coat (Act II, scene vi). In another scene, an enraged Don Torcuato proposes to manhandle Don Saturio. He rushes at him with arms raised, but Saturio, mistaking his intentions, thinks he wants to embrace and so he throws his arms around Torcuato. The scene ends that way, with the wooden Torcuato struggling to free himself from the equally wooden Saturio:

> LUCIANA: Oh! The two of you embraced....
> (Act II, scenes x, xi)

In 1895, *Love's Referee* was staged in Mexico City, and the poet Amado Nervo wrote a brief criticism of it. His thoughts are worth recording here since they typify the nineteenth century criticism of Bretón's plays. Nervo wrote:

The play ... like all those of its author, abounds in gracefulness and winsomeness. The versification has that admirable fluidity that characterizes *El pelo de la dehesa* and in general all the works of Bretón. One leaves the theater still relishing the Attic flavor of that metrical art, embellished at times with easy *esdrújulos* always correct and always attractive.

Beyond that, *Love's Referee* has such a simple and uniform plot that the work might better be considered a gallery of types, perfectly executed....[13]

Like many nineteenth century critics, Nervo wrote largely in generalities.

IV A Sweetheart for the Girl (Un novio para la niña, *1834*)

Larra and Molíns, Bretón's friends and contemporaries, failed to see that *A Sweetheart for the Girl* was a radically different play from *Marcela*. To be sure, it had three suitors and one girl, it had the Moratinianlike theme of *El sí de la niñas,* and like *Marcela* it was polymetrical. But here the resemblance ended. *A Sweetheart for the Girl* is a play of intrigue with many contrivances and a deus ex machina. It condemns the man of money, looks askance at the nineteenth century, waxes melodramatic, preaches a moral at the end, and through a misdirected letter, reveals the truth about a very evil man. One principal character turns *raisonneur* (moralizer) and admits to the role. *A Sweetheart for the Girl* is a forerunner of the *alta comedia* of Tamayo y Baus and López de Ayala in the 1860s and 1870s. It also displays the apparatus of the "well-made play" of Augustin Eugène Scribe (1791-1861).[14]

The young girl Concha compares herself to her pet linnet, who also lives in a cage. She addresses the bird in some cloying verses and then gives it its freedom. She is to be married to one of two boors by an ambitious mother. Her true lover, Don Manuel, is in trouble because three robbers have stolen his month's rent, which he owes her mother, the keeper of a boarding house. Her brother, Don Diego, might have protected her, but he has been absent for twelve years and has not written a letter in the last four. Then enters the worse of the two suitors, Don Donato, reciting verses in praise of money: "What's the use of being a gentleman, / if you don't have money?" (Act I, scene v). Money being a thing of evil, Don Donato is a vulgar, filthy millionaire! The long-lost brother Don Diego now appears, but nobody recognizes him. He has been in a coach accident, and the two ladies who have nursed him turn out to be Manuel's mother and sister! After a quick recognition (the anagnorisis) — "¡Madre mía!" ("Mother") — Diego declares that he will save his sister, Concha.

In Act III, Diego intercepts a letter revealing the machinations of the affected Don Fulgencio, Concha's other suitor. Then he melodramatically employs a series of ruses, frightening away both pretenders. He has Concha marry Manuel, thus repaying his debt to the "two celestial women" who nursed him. In his closing lines, Diego jokingly becomes the *raisonneur,* which seems to be Bretón's way of asking the audience for its much-needed indulgence. *A Sweetheart for the Girl,* whose spirit is scarcely Bretonian, is not one of Marcela's sisters; it has generous heapings of what George Bernard Shaw has called *Sardoodledum*.[15] It begins with a love story, but thereafter reveals more exposition than dramatization of an exceedingly complicated plot.

V *"For the Album of an Actress"*

We digress here for a brief discussion of a poem by Bretón that has a line apparently referring to his *This World, a Farce,* the last of the "twin sisters" named above.

In the nineteenth century, it was customary for a lady to give her album to a gentleman at a party so that he might write in it, perhaps a few verses celebrating her beauty. José María Pereda describes this custom in his novel *Pedro Sánchez:*

As I left ... Luz said to me:
— I know you are a poet and I want you to do me a favor.
....
— Supposing I were a poet — I replied — what favor can I possibly do for you?
—You might honor my album by writing something in it. Her album! At that time the album was in all its glory and splendor. Everybody had an album, and they would send it to the most ordinary man to have him "put something" in it....[16]

Bretón himself wrote a poem called "For the Album of an Actress." This album may not have existed, since there is no record of it, and it seems unlikely that he would write ninety-six, mostly pessimistic, verses for a young female admirer.[17]

The first twenty-one quatrains argue that the world, like the theater, is a farce and that young swains are actors, *farsantes*. Their protestations of love are a ridiculous and empty show, a mockery. Consequently:

> Guard, young girl, thy heart,
> Punish all these actors
> With an eye for an eye, a tooth for a tooth;
> Play the farce on them! Forward!   (*Obras 1883,* V, 233)

And in one quatrain Bretón refers the young actress to one of his own plays, an *exemplum* of his farcical antimatrimonial doctrine:

> Thou must read, dear girl,
> To learn why I argue so,
> My play that's called
> *This World, A Farce.* (*Obras 1883,* V, 233)

Whereas Bretón's first twenty-one quatrains reveal a "peculiar personality ... growing resigned in pessimism," like Juvenal's,[18] the last three quatrains are a *volte-face:*

> But should Pelayo's God
> Decree, oh graceful maid,
> That thou changest thy mask for a housecoat,
> A coat it will be, and that's all.
> Mother Nature rules
> More than Rojas and Terence,
> And on such a bland sweet voice
> Who dares to impose silence?
> Although pretty and alluring,
> Thou art a human being,
> And thou wilt have thy day [Y tendrás tu cuarto de hora]
> Like every good young maid.[19] (*Obras 1883,* V, 235)

These quatrains, which oppose the previous twenty-one (in summary, "Play the farce on them!"), somehow symbolize Bretón's own life and theater. He may write a Juvenalian satire on love and marriage, he may even wear at times a bitter pagan mask, but when all is said and done he believes in the order created by Pelayo's God, which ordains marriage. Bretón was not one to moralize in the fashion of Fernán Caballero or Luis Coloma, or to write "high plays" about good and evil, in the fashion of Tamayo y Baus; but neither did he question traditional Spanish religious traditions. These institutions would be questioned shortly after him, historically by the novelist Galdós, and philosophically by the Generation of 1898, with Unamuno, Baroja, and Valle in the lead.

One should note again that the first part of Bretón's album poem cites his play *This World, A Farce* (1835), and that the second part contains the title of another play, "Y tendrás tu cuarto de hora" — one of Bretón's plays is called *El cuarto de hora* (*Her Fateful Moment,* 1840). It behooves us now to study these two works.

VI This World A Farce (Todo es farsa en este mundo, *1835*)

In this comedy, two *farsantes* (the word means *fakers* as well as *actors*) seek the hand of a young girl. These *farsantes* personify the thought of "For the Album of an Actress," although Bretón's play has a winsomeness altogether wanting in the poem: its wit is not bitter but humorous.

Every comedy by Bretón offers something for the culturally aware reader, who will remember in *This World, A Farce* the presence of the Carlists and the description of a new cafeteria style restaurant (Act I, scene v). This comedy also contains one of the classic sayings of the Spanish language. Don Rufo Jaramago ("Hedge-mustard") has been a Carlist, but now supports Isabel II, thinking she has given him a new government job. He has a job ... and then he doesn't; he is suddenly unemployed, a *cesante* under the Spanish spoils system. Will he go back to the Carlists? What are his politics?:

RUFO:	Before I was a fool,
	and now I am ... now I am, nobody!
EUSTOQUIA:	You said that our country....
RUFO:	The jobless have no country!
	[¡No hay patria para un cesante!] (Act III, scene vi)

"¡No hay patria para un cesante!": the unemployed job-seeker, the man without a country! The expression has a special meaning in Spanish, where the *cesante* is a most prominent figure in nineteenth century literature.[20]

VII Her Fateful Moment (El cuarto de hora, *1842*)

In *Her Fateful Moment,*[21] the pretty, alluring girl is Carolina, wooed by the "opulent Andalusian," Marchena, and secretly loved by the poet-artist and family secretary, Ortiz.

Ortiz begins to disclose his love, but Carolina merely laughs at him, and at Marchena as well. The latter, imitating Moreto's Golden Age play *Treat Disdain With Disdain* (see Act II, scene iv), employs the ruse of flattering Carolina's affected maid, Petra, and her fifty year old aunt, Doña Liboria, who believes his lies. Disdained now, angry, and chastened, Carolina starts to change:

> He would not be swaggering
> if I were not a coquette.
> But now I find myself
> in a crisis very grave;

> and I am losing tranquility,
> and my soul tells me —
> shouting with might and main —
> that I have to love somebody. (Act V, scene i)

And Carolina keeps changing until she experiences "her fateful moment," in the last act, when she promises to marry Ortiz. The two *farsantes,* actors and fakers, Marchena and Petra, end up looking ridiculous. The fifty year old Doña Liboria is sadder and wiser:

> I sinned too, confound it!
> but who, my girl, is free
> of a fateful moment?
> In my self-esteem I regret
> the disillusion I must bemoan;
> but truly, it's disgusting to think
> that someone as old as I
> should dream of those little fateful moments. Act V, scene ix)

Nature has ordained love as the privilege of young girls, who have beautiful eyes and figures and turn a young man's head. Only the young have fateful moments; an older woman should know that.

The Madrid public enjoyed this kind of play. Prior to its appearance in December of 1840, Bretón had lost favor in many quarters; his circumstantial play, *La Ponchada,* had been hissed, and for political reasons he was dismissed as librarian in the National Library. He felt persecuted; responsible authorities had not come to his aid. He was depressed and on the verge of emigrating to a foreign country, but, in the words of his nephew, Cándido Bretón y Orozco: "What made him desist from this plan was the great success enjoyed by the play called *El cuarto de hora,* which was shown in the Príncipe theater on December 10, 1840. The author was overjoyed to see that he had won back the public's favor, and modestly and gallantly attributing his triumph to the fine acting of Doña Matilde Díez, he dedicated a *romance* of thanks to this famous actress...."[22]

When Bretón was his own author, when he wrote the kind of play he was famous for, such as *Marcela* or *El cuarto de hora,* he had the Madrid audiences at his feet.

CHAPTER 6

Figure, Coquetry, Gallantry, and Marriage

AS young men, Bretón and other members of his literary group, the *Parnasillo*,[1] frequented the house of a certain Dr. Vives, who had three beautiful daughters. Besides being beautiful and talented, these young ladies "it would seem, also had a good measure of requisite coquetry,"[2] so much so that everyone was writing them love poetry. Ventura de la Vega wrote verses to Laura, Juan de la Pezuela to Rosaura, and Bretón to Mariquita, the Silvia of his Anacreontics, she of the blue eyes, pink cheeks, and blonde hair. Le Gentil, describing this part of Bretón's life, wrote:

We do not know the outcome of this pastoral episode, conducted in the fashion of Meléndez Valdés. And let us not try to make up a denouement. With melancholic obstinacy, Bretón, detained in the south of Spain, on the shores of the Guadalquivir, will continue to sing to Silvia; he will retain a preference for romantic scenes that is surprising in a humorist; finally, his theater will be the deification of coquetry. He would have understood this subtle game less clearly if he himself had not risked getting burned in it. When his friends and acquaintances attended the première of *Marcela,* on December 30, 1831, they could assign a real name to each character. The elegant *marivaudage* of Bretón is not a product of his fantasy, but the conversation he remembered of three select young ladies, who were courted by the flower of the *Parnasillo*.[3]

Is Bretón's theater the deification of coquetry, as Le Gentil would have it? There can be no doubt that coquetry abounds in his plays. Can his style be called an "elegant *marivaudage*," that is, "a delicate and exquisite banter about details of feeling?" Some of his plays bear similarities to Marivaux's *Les fausses confidences,* which he had translated early in his career.[4]

68

Figure, Coquetry, Gallantry, and Marriage 69

Before discussing coquetry (*coquetería*) in Bretón's theater, it is convenient to discuss the concept of figure, or *talle*.

I *A Vision of Love:* Talle

Joseph Addison wrote: "Sunday clears away the rust of the whole week not only as it refreshes in their mind the notions of religion, but as it puts both the sexes upon appearing in their most agreeable forms, and exerting all such qualities as are apt to give them a figure in the eye of the village." Addison's "both ... sexes ... appearing in their most agreeable forms" is an apt definition of Bretón's theater.[5]

Bretón's plays constantly refer to a woman's *talle* — her waist, figure, or form. No other image appears in his plays as often as this. Sometimes other words are used for *talle*, for example, "*cuerpo agraciado,*" "*sus nobles prendas*" (*The Two Nephews*), "*su cara y cuerpo*" (*It's Back to Madrid for Me*), "*cuerpo celestial*" (*Marcela*), "*¡qué talle, qué formas!*" (*The Recluses*). A woman's figure attracts men, and among them one man in particular. Lest this thought seem to be commonplace (viz., women have a beautiful form, therefore they attract men), Bretón not only gathered it from his observations of human nature, he also saw it staged in the plays of Marivaux, Scribe, Monvel, Rojas Zorrilla, Tirso, Moratín, and Lope de Vega. The Golden Age comedies he adapted to the nineteenth century stage are filled with the image of *talle*, especially the comedies of Tirso de Molina.[6] In one play, *The Editor Responsible,* Bretón has a seamstress give the exact measurements of a woman's waist:

> ANA: But this skirt is
> endless! Nine pieces of cloth...,
> and to fit the waist [y para abarcar el talle]
> just a little more than half a *vara!* (Act I, scene i)

A *vara* is eighty-four centimeters, or thirty-five inches, which brings the lady's waist to about eighteen inches. The subsequent conversation of the seamstress suggests that this measurement is less than average, and therefore admirable.

The word *talle* is also applied to men, although less frequently. See, for example, *It's Back To Madrid For Me,* Act II, scene viii:

Don Felipe de Villegas.
. . . .
The very same. Good-looking,
his complexion somewhat swarthy,
but with a fine pink color;
a well-formed waist [*buen talle*], graceful presence,
handsome face, black eyes,
and so..., a modest manner
and upright....

A person with such a good form (*talle*) seems necessarily a man of probity, one who will win the girl's hand and heart at the end. He is an offspring of Cervante's heroes an heroines in *The Exemplary Novels,* with their noble blood. Thus, a good form is a corollary of a man's coming from good family or bloodstock. Conversely, a man can have a bad form, such as the dandy Agapito, who cuts "una figura triste" (*Marcela,* Act III, scene ix).

The first acceptance of *talle*, then, is corporeal. It means that a woman, or a man, has a fine body, one that will attract the opposite sex. This is why the *cuerpo celestial* of Marcela inspires men to love her; literally, "it strikes them with an arrow" ("la viuda te ha flechado" [Act II, scene vii]; "Ese cuerpo ha dado a todos / flechazo" [Act II, scene i]).[7]

II Talle *as Presence and as Idea*

The second acceptance of *talle* in Bretón's theater goes beyond the corporeal to the presence of a person, which includes spiritual qualities. We have already seen a suggestion of this in the description of Don Felipe de Villegas quoted above. When applied to a man, *talle* usually has the connotation Covarrubias gave it in his Thesaurus of 1611: "A man of good form, is the same as saying a gentleman and a man of manners."[8] In *The Newspaper*, Fabricio cannot understand how a discreet young man, who naturally has a good figure, can fall for an ungainly woman:

How can a young man,
who is discreet, has a fine figure,
and what is more, is loved
by such a beautiful girl,
so cute, ... how can he fall
for a small tub like that?   (Act II, scene iii)

Figure, Coquetry, Gallantry, and Marriage

Discretion and a fine figure should go together in a man, and he will be loved by a beautiful girl ("muchacha tan pulcra"), "pulcra" also meaning a girl of good habits.

In *The Bodily Senses,* graciousness and wit accompany physical beauty, and good taste a soft figure:

> A woman, good heavens!
> with her grace and charm,
> with her divine beauty
> has captured my will.
> . . . .
> How can I put into words that
> good taste, that soft figure [*blando talle*]... (Act I, scene vii)

A good form or figure and fine spiritual qualities thus go together. Similarly, a woman of "celestial form" will also be a woman of "pure candor" rather than "lewdness";

> And though she takes not care
> to conceal her celestial form,
> 'Tis simply candor in her
> what in others would be lewdness.
> ("Mi Dama," *Obras 1883,* V, 262)

This "pure candor" in Bretón's lady is the same graceful sprightliness (*desenvoltura*) that Cervantes sees in Preciosa, the little gypsy, and other heroines.[9]

Finally, a beautiful form (*talle*) is a source of poetry:

Si tu faz donosa	If one dare look
Se atreve a mirar	At your winsome face
No hay rosa	There's no rose
Que hermosa	That beautiful
Se pueda llamar.	Can be named.
Ni Venus te iguala;	Nor is Venus your peer;
Que la hace gemir,	For she will moan,
Zagala,	Lass,
Tu gala	On seeing
Tu dulce reír.	Your glory, your lovely smile.
. . . .	. . . .
Y ufana te admira	And proud to admire you
Cual reina de Abril	Like April's queen

Mi lira	Is my lyre
Tu talle gentil.	By your graceful form.

("A Lola En Sus Días," *Obras 1883,* p. 135)

A winsome face, lovely smile, and graceful form (*talle*) all give rise to lyrical poetry.

Whereas a woman's form readily captivates a man, her own falling in love is somewhat different. She has something within her resembling a platonic idea, a fantasy, a spiritual form representing a man, and when she sees the *talle* of the flesh-and-blood man who conforms to this idea, she falls hopelessly in love.[10] This is the fateful moment, her *cuarto de hora* (see Chapter 5). The best example of this vision of love comes from the beautiful *zarzuela, El novio pasado por agua* (*The Parboiled Fiancé,* 1852):

ELENA: Mi exaltada fantasía	Did my exalted fantasy
¿no formó el grato diseño	not form the pleasing model
del que solo para dueño	of him alone
anhelaba el alma mía?	who my soul longed for as lord?

(Act I, scene vi)

Thus a woman's form, her body and manner, will attract several suitors, and if one of them has the proper form and manner he will be her master. In th play *Mocedades, Youthful Adventures,* Casilda calls Joaquín her *dulce dueño,* her *unico dueño* (Act III, scene iii), and in *The Two Nephews,* Doña Catalina observes:

> But finally the time has come
> to give my hand, as a prize
> for his affection, to him who
> is already master of my heart.[11]   (Act V, scene iv)

Finally, the union of two *talles,* of a man and a woman, is an act of nature. In the most charming of Bretón's one act plays, *Entre santa y santo* (*Between A Saintly Man and Woman,* 1862) written when he was almost seventy, the young widow Doña Engracia holds dear the memory of her deceased husband and plans to enter a convent, whereas Don Modesto Bonifaz has been deceived in love and has little use for all women. As they ride in a stagecoach together, the wall between them gradually breaks down. At play's end, in a rainstorm, with Engracia's maid as witness, they call each other *esposo* and *esposa* and set off on foot together for a town. Heaven smiles on their union:

Figure, Coquetry, Gallantry, and Marriage 73

MANUELA [the maid]: Here the guest is provident
　　Nature, whose imperium is not easily resisted,
　　as I've already told you, and especially in the
　　verdant years of youth. (scene xi)

In scene i, Manuela had said to Engracia, who was planning to bury herself in a convent: "Nature also has her prescriptions, and they are usually quite effective." *Talle,* nature's chief prescription, is most effective.[12]

III *Coquetry*

According to Bretón's plays, every woman is by nature a coquette. In *The Newspaper* (Act II, scene ii), Agustín tells the actress that if he were a poet he would write a role for her, perhaps that of an empress. She says she would prefer the role of a coquette, and when he asks: "Are you one?" she answers: "Every girl portrays that role." In *The Two Nephews* (Act II, scene iii), the virtuous Catalina tells her lover Cándido that although she may seem to be a coquette, she has a pure heart and sound head; she can distinguish the wheat from the chaff, and she scorns the ridiculous Adonis who is wooing her. And in *The School of Wives* (Act II, scene viii), Antonia tells Carmen why every woman, no matter what her state in life, must be a coquette:

> In brief, all women need,
> no matter what
> their state in life,
> (and married women, even more!)
> a bit of that innocent
> artifice, of that gift
> known as coquetry,
> which pleases men and God
> when moderately used
> with pious intention.
> . . . .
> 　　I have fewer
> charms than you, and I'm a coquette
> and my husband adores me.

Nature grants a woman a form, a *talle,* and if she adds to nature's gift some flirtatious art of her own she will attract and hold the man she is destined for, whose image preexists in her fantasy.

Not all coquettes are the same, however. In one of his articles (*Obra dispersa,* p. 207), Bretón mentions "false coquettes," those who attend masked balls[13] and stand in contrast to the virtuous Catalina and Antonia of *The School of Wives.* And in his introduction to the 1850 edition of his *Obras* he had this to say: "Thus I have reproduced, for example, I don't know how often, the character of the *coquette,* and quite a few times that of the faker ... but not all my coquettes are of the same kind nor do they appear in the same circumstances, and not all my deceivers are cast in the same mold...."[14] In Bretón there are basically two types of coquette, the one natural and pleasing and wholesome, the other false and calculating and unwholesome. Thus in his poem "Mi Dama" he tells us that his lady is a good person whereas many other women are not: "'Tis simply candor in her/what in others would be lewdness." (*Obras 1883,* V, 262) And in the *comedia-zarzuela, The Loners* (Act I, scene iv), Lucía explicitly refers to innocent coquetry:

> You must have formed,
> like all us women, an
> ideal type of man....
> ....
> But you can cleverly look for occasions,
> or chance meetings. A woman looks at
> others and gets them to look at her. In
> short, there are harmless wiles and
> innocent coquetry.[15]

Women keep in their fantasy an ideal type of man, and although the social initiative is forbidden them, they can by innocent flirtation make sure that one particular man notices them. The girl Mariana may say she does not want to be a coquette, and that there's no such thing as an ideal type (she does say this, in other verses), but actions speak louder than words. Mariana, who has been melancholic and misanthropic, acknowledges her error at play's end (*The Loners,* Act I, scenes xxiii, xxiv).

The best Bretonian portrait of the arrant coquette (*fieffée coquette:* see note 12 of this chapter) appears in scene vi of the one act play *Water Over the Dam* (*A lo hecho pecho,* 1844), where Tadeo describes his deceased wife, Julia, to his brother. She was a confirmed coquette. Educated in the great wide world, she was the astonishment of Madrid, and:

Su talle era el figurín	Her figure was the perfect model
que estudiaban las modistas.	which dressmakers used to study.

After Tadeo's wedding, everyone could approach Julia but him, except on those days she reserved for shopping. A coquette before marriage, she was an archcoquette after it.[16]

IV *Gallantry*

Webster's Dictionary defines *gallantry* as "Civility or polite attention to ladies." The Dictionary of the Royal Spanish Academy (1947 ed.) gives as one meaning of *galantería* "Gracia y elegancia que se advierte en la forma o figura de algunas cosas" ("Grace and elegance to be observed in the form or figure of some things").

In the spring of 1830 Mr. Henry David Inglis left England for a year's travel in Spain. The following year he published his two volume work, *Spain in 1830*, in which he observed:

Every Spanish house has its *tertulia;* and every man, woman, girl, and boy, is a member of one *tertulia* or another. The introduction to the *tertulia* begins at a very early age. I have seen boys who, in any country, would have been in a school-room, or at play, present themselves regularly at the *tertulia,* and throwing off the character of boys, act the part of grown-up men.... The foundation of the *tertulia* is gallantry; — here it is that the Spanish woman, after having reaped a harvest of admiration on the Prado, retires to receive that nearer homage which is prized still higher; and here it is that the Spaniard makes his prelude to future conquest. Gallantry is the business of every Spaniard's life; his object in attending the *tertulia* is to practice it; and his principal study, therefore, is that frivolous and gallant conversation that is essential in the first place to captivate the attention of the Spanish woman. The Spanish ladies, with all their agreeable wit and affability, are ignorant almost beyond belief....[17]

Given Inglis's observation, Bretón's theater is rather like a series of *tertulias,* where young women came to be seen and young men to play the gallant. His women are not as ignorant as Inglis's, or Moratín's, since they are widows with experience;[18] nor is their conversation, which often takes place between two earnest people hopeful of marrying each other, always frivolous. But picture a gathering with people of various ages, the young lovers being generally good and the old parents being generally meddlesome, with a young dandy or boor trying to disrupt the lovers and an old uncle trying to unite them against dandy, boor, and parents, with pleasant coquetry and gallantry appearing in most scenes, with a humorous servant animating the action — picture this and you will have a good idea of a Bretonian play.

In *Marcela,* Act I, scene viii, Don Martín utters words of gallantry to the young widow, and after some nonsense on the part of the dandy, Agapito, she defines the gallant man:

> The refined man,
> sophisticated, with good upbringing,
> is gallant with the ladies,
> and, as long as he offends not
> their modesty, if he courts them
> he fulfills his obligation.

Since none of her three suitors measures up to this standard of gallantry, she rejects them.

In his acceptance speech before the Spanish Royal Academy of the Language, in 1837, Bretón makes a special reference to gallantry. He has been arguing that verse is superior to prose in the composition of comedies, and he offers scenes of gallantry as an example: "It seems that scenes of gallantry, which are most common in the *comedia,*[19] require more than any other scenes the easy-moving sprightliness of the *redondilla.* Here is a most beautiful declaration of love from Montalbán's comedy *Cumplir con su obligación.*"[20] The scene Bretón quotes from Juan Pérez de Montalbán (1602-1638), in which Don Juan confesses his love to Camila, resembles many scenes from Bretón's own theater, for example, Act II, scene iii, of *The Two Nephews,* where Cándido and Catalina discreetly unfold their love. Bretón is never far removed from the Golden Age *comedia.*

Although coquetry and gallantry are recognizable and susceptible of description, Bretón leaves room for the mystery of love. No matter how much literature is written about love, one never arrives at its terminus. The subject is inexhaustible. Witness the following conversation from Act I, scene ii, of *To the Letter (Al pie de la letra):*

> AQUILINO: *Your conscience is bothering you!*
> *You love that fop!*
> ISABEL: *There's no such love. What a bore!*
> *Friendship...*

| AQUILINO: | *Always becomes ambiguous between a man and woman. And yours was not born yesterday, but long before that.* |

Who will draw the line between friendship and erotic love? In his aphoristic verse, "Friendship ... / Always becomes ambiguous / between a man and woman," Bretón has pointed to the most important mystery of the human psyche. He will not attempt to define it.[21]

V Marriage, And A Theory Concerning Cervantes

The goal of good form and figure and presence, of coquetry and gallantry, of the entire Bretonian "amorous merry-go-round,"[22] is marriage. Greedy mothers, dowry seekers, poetasters, fops, lascivious coquettes, lechers, and others may cast a pall over the goal, but it stands supreme, and in most plays the young lovers achieve it. The Bretonian picture then is clear; form (*talle*) leads to coquetry-gallantry, which leads to marriage. The girl of the beautiful eyes wins the man of noble form.[23]

Bretón's vision of love bears a striking resemblance to Cervantes's vision in *The Exemplary Novels,* specifically, *The Little Gypsy* and *The Illustrious Kitchen Maid.* The two *coqueterías* of Bretón, the innocent and the guileful, correspond to the two *desenvolturas* of Cervantes, the pure and the lascivious.

Preciosa, the little gypsy, has a noble presence. She is celebrated for her beauty, gracefulness, discretion, wit, purity, neatness, and natural gifts such as singing and dancing, which she does far better than any other girl. She has emerald eyes and golden hair. All the men who see her are amazed, astounded, enraptured, suspended, stunned. Perhaps her most attractive charm, distinguishing her from all other women, is her *desenvoltura:* "Not that, gallant sir — replied Preciosa —; know you that I must always have unencumbered liberty, without the affliction of jealousy disturbing or suffocating it; and understand that I will not take too much liberty and that even from afar you will surely see that my modesty is the equal of my forwardness [*desenvoltura*]."[24] Preciosa is an outgoing, cheerful, sprightly, graceful girl, always at ease in dealing with others. As far as men are concerned, she has a natural coquetry that will make them all fall in love with her.

Don Juan de Cárcamo falls deeply in love with Preciosa, who in turn is attracted by his form: "While the young gentleman was saying this, Preciosa was looking at him attentively, and without doubt his words and his figure musn't have seemed bad to her [ni sus razones ni su talle]." In brief, Don Juan sees Preciosa's superior form and *desenvoltura;* and she sees his form, his *razones* and *talle.* They contract a two year engagement, and finally, marriage. There is, to be sure, a less admirable *desenvoltura,* a looseness or boldness rather than a forwardness, an immodest self-assurance corresponding to Bretón's guileful coquetry. The lascivious Juana Carducha, "somewhat more loose than beautiful," is smitten with love for Don Juan de Cárcamo. She proposes marriage to him but "would deliver herself up to his will without matrimonial bonds." Bretón's concepts parallel those of Cervantes insofar as the two *coqueterías* may lead to marriage or to serious trouble,[25] and the two *desenvolturas* will do the same.

VI *The Charge of Superficiality*

Nineteenth century criticism set up a dichotomy between Bretón's jocoseness on the one hand and dramatic profundity on the other. He was noted for his festive air; ergo, he was not, indeed he could not be, profound. In short, his theater was superficial.

An example of this attitude can be seen in the words of Antonio Ferrer del Río (1814-1872): "Unquestionably, the ability to entertain spectators with a slow-moving action shows merit, the author supplying with comic wit what is lacking in interest and intrigue; we ourselves would prefer more complication, because in this way Mr. Bretón de los Herreros would make his subjects more profound."[26] The dean of nineteenth century Spanish critics, Marcelino Menéndez Pelayo (1856-1912), expressed a similar, though more generous, opinion:

Bretón is a mine of inexhaustible humor, and he always provides in the mirth of his dialogue what it lacks in transcendence and poetic substance. He has portrayed the middle class of his day, although he stretches traits to the point of caricature. Most fortunate in his selection of subjects, he is not in general equally fortunate in his manner of developing them. In many cases he sees the human and dramatic truth, but only scratches the surface. From this sin of superficiality, the only serious one he has, which is well made up for by excellence in other areas, one must always exempt some works of his of exceptional quality, for example, *Muérete ¿y verás!,*

La batelera de Pasajes, El pelo de la dehesa, ¿Quién es ella?, and a couple of others he has written more painstakingly.[27]

The one critic who perceived the flaw in this critical dichotomy was Juan Martínez Villergas (1816–1894), who wrote in his study of Bretón:

This preoccupation I am complaining about is that of looking at jocose works with a certain disdain even though they have merit, and of reserving praise for serious and pompous compositions, although as Proudhon says, they make up for the emptiness of ideas with bombastic words.... We see mediocre people pride themselves on their importance, which only their friends, fools like them, admire, and we see them scorn all inspiration that takes on the festive form. And they say with a petulant air: "That is a tavern style."[28]

Perhaps the question of superficiality can be approached in two ways. In the first place, there are authors who deliberately touch the surface (or *superficie*) of things, who delight in taking an aspect of something and portraying it in their own way. An example of this surface art is Peruvian history in the hands of Ricardo Palma, in his *Tradiciones peruanas.* Or one may recall Spanish history in the hands of Pedro Antonio de Alarcón, in the *Historietas nacionales.* One might even extend this argument to authors such as Cervantes and Calderón, for not all of Cervantes's *entremeses* have quixotic greatness, and Calderón wrote *mojigangas* as well as *Life is a Dream.* There is ample room in this world for superficial art, the art of the surface, which has but one requisite: that it be well done. If it is well done, it will entertain.[29]

Secondly, one might consider the question of *fondo* and *forma,* of subject and form.[30] An author may take a serious, profound subject and write a bombastic play about it, so that the subject itself becomes empty of ideas (see Martínez Villergas: "they make up for the emptiness of ideas with bombastic words"). This argument will hold for many plays written by the generation succeeding Bretón; a comparison of his *Marcela* with Manuel Tamayo y Baus' *Del dicho al hecho* and Victorien Sardou's "well-made play," *Les pattes de Mouche,* will demonstrate that a simple play is preferable to a complicated drama if the latter lacks artistic inspiration. Ferrer del Río's longed-for greater "complication" and more "interest and intrigue" do not alone and of themselves make for better theater.

If we apply the criterion of superficiality in its first sense, namely, that of surface art, Bretón's name deserves to be ranked with those of Palma, Alarcón, the Rivas of the *Romances históricos,* the *costumbristas* of the nineteenth century, and others. His theater is filled with many memorable images of Madrid from the 1820s to the 1850s; he is justly recognized as a fine *costumbrista* and the author of a new comedy of manners.

If the second criterion be taken, a distinction must be made between *fondo* and *forma.* It is factually incorrect to say, as many critics have done, that Bretón did not treat profound subjects and did not vary them. He wrote plays on the love of men and women, the newspaper world, censorship, "ministerial weaknesses," the spoils system, the Carlist war, the War of the Spanish Succession, a medieval legend, the misogynistic Quevedo, the theme of Calderón's *Mayor of Zalamea,* gambling, the Moratinian vision of marriage, independence and the uprising of Riego, phrenology, magic, country life and city life, and other subjects. Perhaps the critics meant that the most characteristic or typical Bretonian play is not profound, *typical* meaning a comedy in which young people fall in love and finally choose a spouse. But since even such a comedy will include Bretón's vision of love, described earlier in this chapter, it is difficult to see how his theater can be considered superficial in its entirety.[31]

CHAPTER 7

Three Major Plays

IN his summary of Bretón's theater, Marcelino Menéndez Pelayo wrote the following opinion: "From this sin of superficiality ... one must always exempt some works of exceptional quality, for example, *Muérete ¡y verás!, La batelera de Pasajes, El pelo de la dehesa, ¿Quién es ella?,* and a pair of others he has written more painstakingly."[1] The present chapter will discuss three of these four plays of "exceptional quality," and a sequel to one of them, in chronological order: *Die and You Will See!* (*Muérete ¡y verás!,* 1837), *The Country Bumpkin* (*El pelo de la dehesa,* 1840), and *The Ferry-girl From Pasajes,* (*La batelera de Pasajes,* 1842). *Show Me The Woman* (*¿Quién es ella?,* 1849), the drama about Philip IV and Quevedo, will be studied in a separate chapter, along with Bretón's historical dramas.

I   Die and You Will See, (Muérete ¡y verás!, *1837*)

Although *Marcela* (1831) was Bretón's most successful play, *Die and You Will See!* was his personal favorite.[2] After its première on April 26, 1837, the audience called Bretón to the stage amidst loud applause, for the first time in his life. Their tribute was in effect a poetic coronation.[3]

What sort of a play was *Die and You Will See!?* Le Gentil assigned it a political character and saw Bretón "making himself the interpreter of loyalist sentiments aroused by the civil war." Hartzenbusch called it a "comedy of serious thought, one of the best of our day."[4] Chaskin speaks of Romantic satire in *Die and You Will See!* and says that the third act, "The Burial" ("El Entierro"), "is a clever parody of a Romantic drama."[5] Opinion differed over the source of the plot, Molíns seeing the origin in Dumas's *Catherine Howard,* Le Gentil in Scribe's *Inconsolables.*[6]

Although *Die and You Will See!* unquestionably has a mirthful air, there is reason for seeing political gravity and serious thought in it as did Molíns and Hartzenbusch, both of them close friends of Bretón. In a footnote to his drama about a misogynous Francisco de Quevedo, Bretón reminds the reader that "in his long career he had shown that if in general as a comic poet he had preferred to make people laugh, other springs of the human heart were not unknown to him."7 This was not the first time that he, Bretón, was trying his mettle in producing "the sentimental, the picturesque, the pathetic, or even the terrible." *Show Me The Woman*, (*¿Quién es ella?*, the play about Quevado) has a diversity of tones, and so do eight other plays, amongst them *Die and You Will See!* Thus he himself suggests that *Die and You Will See!*, although it will make people laugh, has a further design; if they laugh they will be both enjoying themselves and responding to a serious purpose of the author.

II *The Plot of* Die and You Will See!

The play has a quasi-religious plot. In the tradition of the novel and some Romantic dramas of the time, the four acts have titles, which read like an abbreviated Stations of the Cross: I, The Leavetaking; II, Death; III, The Burial; IV, Resurrection. In the first act, Lieutenant Pablo Yagüe takes leave of his fiancée and friends to fight the Carlists in Cataluña; Second Lieutenant Matías Calanda accompanies him. In Act II, Matías returns alone, announcing Pablo's death in battle, and he steals his sweetheart, Jacinta. In Act III, Pablo returns from the dead and reveals himself only to the loyal, virtuous Isabel and to the miserly loan shark, Don Elías.[8] Act IV brings the burlesque resurrection of Pablo and day of judgement, on which hypocrites are more severely punished than other malefactors.

Although *Die and You Will See!* has a quasi-religous tone, there is no evidence to show that Bretón was engaged in any sort of homily on the one hand or religious parody on the other. The religious air of the play comes from Romanticism itself, which always displayed an interest in religion, metaphysics, the invisible world, human destiny, salvation, a mysterious man, his death, interment, and even his resurrection. Don Pablo was not the only literary figure to attend his own funeral.[9] Beyond the story of Pablo Yagüe, the man who allegedly died and came back to learn what life was all about, *Die and You Will See!* provides a good picture of the civil war of the 1830s and also of Spanish society; for example, the newspapers, the militia, the blind newscriers, a barber, a notary, the dandies, a coquette, a moneylender, a patriot, a selfish citizen avoiding his duties, a dance, music, the pealing of bells, a funeral, a middle class house, and the hustle and bustle of the street. It is a fine example of the Bretonian *comedia de costumbres*.[10]

III *The Characters*

Die and You Will See! is rich in humorous characters, the most outstanding of which are the usurer, Don Elías, and the pessimistic egoist, Don Froilán. These are two of the best roles in all of Bretón's theater. Elías is an *usurero bergante,* a rascally loan shark who will do anything to pocket a coin, even when purchasing a newspaper for a friend from a blind man (Act II, scene v). His favorite word, *económico* or *economizar,* which he comically repeats over and over,[11] is the basis of his marriage proposal to Isabel:

> I love you. More concise
> no lover could be,
> and my economy is such that
> I speak not more than is needed.   (Act II, scene iii)

Unaware that his money lust is a vice, Elías acts and speaks awkwardly; he is a figure of fun resembling the *gracioso* of Lope's day.[12] He often advances the action of the play, and all in all he is likeable, perhaps because his vice is a natural one.[13] The most humorous scenes occur when Elías endeavors to get Pablo to sign a receipt for the three thousand *reales* he has borrowed, at only "twenty per cent ... every four months." Pablo, who is constantly interrupted by other persons, does not get to sign the note; after his alleged death Elías prays at his funeral:

> Oh Virgin Mother, you who pray
> for us .. creditors!
> Does an insolvent corpse deserve
> such devotional prayer?   (Act III, scene xi)

One aspect of Elías's character requires clarification. Mazade, writing in 1847, has said: "One should not forget a grotesque figure of the *juif,* this don Elías who had loaned money at high interest rates to the young militiaman so he could outfit himself, and who bewails his loss." And J. A. Corey, writing in 1972, makes the following statement: "The other character is the Jewish moneylender, Elías. If any progress had been made in Spain to combat hatred of the Jews, it is not apparent in this work."[14]

Elías, however, in spite of his ancient biblical name, is really a Christian (like Galdós' usurers Doña Perfecta and Torquemada, who were to appear on the literary scene some fifty years later). He prays to the *Virgen del Pilar,* the *Virgen Santísima,* and the *Virgen Madre;* he naturally speaks of *responsos* and *kyries;* he proposes marriage to the Christian, Isabel; he constantly uses Church Latin (*per istam, laus deo, parce mihi*), and on the night of Pablo Yagüe's funeral he takes charge of the "funeral honors." Perhaps the supreme irony of Spanish history lies in this: the stereotype Jew turns out to be an Old Christian!

Another irony may be perceived in the name of the play's gloomy prophet, who is not Elías, as one might expect, but the unlikely Froilán. The latter shares the laurels of the comedy with the miserly Elías. He is made of bad stuff:

> Do you know that Don Froilán
> is a bad one, he is?
> The egoistic augur
> they call him in Zaragoza. (Act III, scene vii)

Froilán foretells the future to suit himself: "es agorero por disculpar su egoísmo." He is lazy and would not lift a finger to help a friend; he is moreover, an aphoristic pessimist: "Think the worst and you'll be right, / according to the proverb." (Act I, scene iv) Froilán refuses to attend the funeral service of Don Pablo, who died intestate: "Was his name worth all that? / Two interments for a man / who died without a will!" (Act III, scene v). But when a ruse by the living Pablo makes him think he is the only heir, this "beetle-browed, frowning augur" undergoes an extraordinary metamorphosis and becomes all sweetness and light: he is Pablo's grieving heir — "¡Lo soy (heredero) a mi pesar!" Finally, after Pablo's miraculous resurrection and Froilán's loss of inheritance, everyone laughs at him.

It becomes apparent now that Froilán is not only a figure of fun like Elías; he almost steals the show. Before Pablo goes off to war in Act I, he advises him to stay home:

> Useless courage! Useless

Three Major Plays 85

> patriotism! the die
> is already cast. Poor nation!
> It will moan again a slave.
> ....
> The heavens
> forsake us... We have no country! (Act I, scene viii)[15]

Froilán is the "agorero por disculpar su egoísmo": he predicts a dark future to serve his own ends. He is the antipatriot. He is so foul his skin is yellow (Act II, scene xii).[16] His code is "Me myself alone" (Mi individuo y nada más"). He is an actor, a faker, who assumes tragic airs:

> ELÍAS: While don Froilán is parodying
> Quintana's tragedy,
> please sign. (Act I, scene viii)

Even the miser, Elías, cannot suffer him.

The key to Froilán's important position in the play is a verse by Pablo, who has just returned from the dead to find that all his friends have forgotten him, especially his fiancée Jacinta:

> PABLO: (I ought to go up
> and tell that faithless woman....
> But more than she, her
> brother annoys me. (Act III, scene vii)

Jacinta's brother is Froilán. *Die and You Will See!* — you will see how all the Froilanes, all the hypocrites forsake you. Pablo calls Froilán "a big hypocrite" (Act III, scene xiii), and a lady says of him, "What hypocrisy!" (Act IV, scene viii). Finally Elías, in his own humorous way, defines the nature of Froilán:

> It was an act of very bad faith
> for you, laughing at my abstinence,
> to eat up, besides the inheritance,
> what I had economized.
> You were not the one who deserved
> such joy, you soul of Ananias,
> *Tartuffe* ... I say no more.... (Act IV, scene ix)

Die and You Will See! is another way of saying *Tartuffe!*[17] Bretón is satirizing those hypocrites who made a virtue of selfishness during the civil war of 1833-1839.

Brief mention should be made of the other characters. The scenes with the barber in Act III, which resemble Mesonero Romanos's article "El Barbero de Madrid," are memorable comedy, especially the scene with Elías (scene ix). The barbers of the day were known for their garrulousness, but this barber meets his match in the miser, who is fretting about his money. The two men speak at odds, their dialogue being in effect two simultaneous monologues, and finally the barber loses patience:

BARBER:	Enough! Enough!
	Why to cut off the word of a barber!
ELIAS:	But I . . .
BARBER:	Cursed be your species, amen!
	(He goes into the shop and locks it on the
	inside. The bells stop ringing.) (Act III, scene ix)

The pealing church bells had added to the confusion of these two clowns.[18]

The three *lechuguinos* (dandies), Antonio, Lupercio, and Mariano, are well studied in the dissertation of Silvia Chaskin.[19] She sees them as burlesque substitutes for "the gypsies or villagers so commonly found in Romantic plays," who also serve as "a Greek chorus." The three dandies are *holgazanes* (do-nothings, loiterers).

Isabel, the submissive Spanish lady who finally gets her man, is capable of uttering a truly Calderonian quatrain. Addressing the supposedly dead Pablo, she says:

¡Alma a quien el alma di	Soul to whom I gave my soul,
si a las dos nos escuchaste,	if you heard us two,
mira a qué mujer amaste!	look at the woman you loved!
¡Júzgala y júzgame a mí!	Judge her and then judge me!
	(Act II, scene xv)

Isabel does not know the art of coquetry and sham (Act I, scene i). Jacinta, on the other hand, she of the good figure ("aquel despejo, aquel talle" — Act I, scene i) is the fickle woman. She says she doesn't want to be a coquette (Act I, scene v), but her actions belie her words.

Don Pablo Yagüe, the protagonist of the play, is tall and fair.

Three Major Plays

One can picture him with a noble bearing, standing half a head or more above the other characters. He represents loyalty, trust, and patriotic selflessness. He is the kind of man who will put his beloved's picture next to his breast as he goes off to war, and later, tear it up as soon as he learns of her lack of faith. He plays an extraordinary practical joke, a resurrection in a winding sheet, in order to teach the hypocrites a lesson. Not as memorable as Elías or Froilán, his character is best described as one of youthful candor. Don Matías, his false friend, is just the opposite.[20]

IV   *The Metrical Scheme*

In contrast with *Marcela, Die and You Will See!* displays a simplified metrical scheme. With three exceptions, the play consists entirely of *romances* and *redondillas*. In Act II, two brief bulletins and a letter, all of them reporting on the war, are read in prose. The historical sobriety of the bulletins contrasts with the bombast of Don Matías's letter: "On the very field of battle, covered with enemy corpses, I hasten to advise you of the victory of our arms" (Act II, scene viii). Act III, scene viii, is written in *silvas,* a metrical pattern of heptasyllables and hendecasyllables, most of them rhyming in consonance. This meter is considered appropriate for the monologues recited by persons of high rank when they express strong emotions.[21] But Bretón employs it in the humorous scene heretofore mentioned, where the garrulous barber engages in simultaneous monologue with the miser, Elías. The incongruence of meter and meaning is comical:

THE BARBER   (wondering who the mysterious stranger, Don Pablo, can be):

¡Por el alma de Judas!...	By Judas's soul!...
Ahora le prendería,	I'd arrest him now,
a ser alcalde	were I mayor.
Yo quiero su secreto,	I want his secret
no su barba,	not his beard.
y por salir de dudas	and to gain it
consintiera en rapársela de balde.	I'd consent to shave him free.
¡Señor! ¡Qué extraño ente	Lord! What a strange being
es éste, que una sola *Avemaría*	he is, who will not recite
no reza por el alma de un pariente,	a lone *Hail Mary* for the soul of his relative
y luego, si otra lengua	and then, if another's tongue

| a escarnecer se atreve su ceniza, | scorns the dead man's ashes |
| cual si oyera a Luzbel se escandaliza? | he gets mad, as one hearing Lucifer? |

(Act III, scene viii)

This passage is also a parody of Romantic theater, with its mysterious being (the "ente misterioso," such as Don Alvaro in *La fuerza del sino*).

The same *silvas* in the mouth of Don Elías concern his love of economy:

> Oh blind sinners,
> an example learn from ascetic virtue!
> Another would persist in this sweet error,
> But I, not even on the sinful path,
> I give up wise economy. (Act III, scene ix)

Elías invokes the language of a Romantic hero to show his "torment," and his "fatal recollection" of three thousand *reales* loaned without receipt.

The other change in versification occurs in the last scene of the play, when Pablo and Isabel express their love in *quintillas*. The comedy ends, declaring that the world is a farce (*entremés*), and:

> ANTONIO: To learn how to live ...
> ELÍAS: There is nothing like dying ...
> PABLO: And reviving later on.

V Parody: Criticism, Adverse and Reconciling[22]

Many critics have seen in *Die and You Will See!* a parody of Romantic drama. Like the Romantic playwrights, Bretón gives titles to each of the four acts of his play; and in the first act, to fill the audience in on the background on the action, he uses three *lechuguinos* (dandys) rather than the customary gypsies or townsfolk (see, for example, Rivas' *Don Alvaro*). The third act, where Pablo attends his own funeral, has been construed as a play on Espronceda's *Student of Salamanca,* or more broadly, on the story of Don Miguel de Mañara, the profligate nobleman of Seville.[23] Pablo's appearance in a white sheet burlesques another Romantic device, and the use of exclamation marks, ellipses, vows, and words like "angelical" also parodies Romantic drama.[24]

Three Major Plays

Notwithstanding these various mimicries, it cannot be said that *Die and You Will See!* has the same air of total parody as, say, Ramón de la Cruz's *Manolo* (1769) or Pedro Muñoz Seca's *La venganza de don Mendo* (1918).[25] Cruz, mimicking the French-inspired Neoclassical tragedy, bases his parody on the demeaning of persons and places: the characters are chestnut vendors, tavern keepers, market women, thieves, and convicts, seen in action in the low quarter. He also bases it on the contrast of popular and rhetorical language (e.g., the rogues deliver their speeches in lofty hendecasyllables) and on grotesque situations, such as the aping of the *confidante,* the mocking of dramatic unities, and equivocal statement.[26] Comparing *Manolo* to *Die and You Will See!,* one must conclude that the purpose of the former is amusement and parody, perhaps to correct certain Neoclassical abuses, whereas the latter, providing similar amusement and parody, has in addition another goal.

Hartzenbusch, Bretón's close friend, has said that this play is a "comedy of serious thought."[27] Blanco García praises it as a play in which Bretón applied "elements gathered by Romanticism, without falling into its aberrations, as he did unwisely in *Elena*"; *Die and You Will See!* is a "scene of modern customs," in which Bretón "does not fall into the pit of inverisimilitude."[28] The newspaper *El Eco del Comercio* (1837) made an unusual statement in a review article: "In a word, *Die and You Will See!* is what we would dare to call, if the phrase be permitted, the *Romantic comedy,* a happy innovation whose good results have been demonstrated by experience, and for this we sincerely congratulate Mr. Bretón de los Herreros."[29] One ordinarily associates the Romantic theater with tragedies such as *Don Alvaro* (1835), *El trovador* (1836), and *Los amantes de Teruel* (1837), but here the reviewer speaks of a "Romantic comedy." Such a comedy, then, might include customs, a political argument, a traditional argument about love and marriage, coquetry, a comical correction of hypocrisy and greed, some characters resembling *fantoches,* a large cast with blind newshawkers, soldiers, ladies and gentlemen of the middle class, even the entire populace of a town,[30] and, finally, a parody of the Romantic theater itself.

VI The Country Bumpkin (El pelo de la dehesa, *1840*)

Caricature in Spain has two poles. On the one hand, it is the *jaque,* the swaggering braggart of the South; on the other, it is the *baturro,* the rustic from Zaragoza.[31]

The Catalan was not as insolent as most of his countrymen in the same line of work; the Riojano didn't pretend to be frank or unpolished; and the Andalusian didn't try to be funny.[32]

On February 23, 1840, four days after the opening of *The Country Bumpkin,*[33] the actor Juan Lombía wrote a letter to Miguel Agustín Príncipe: "I am going to tell you one of the greatest joys I have had since becoming an actor. Don Manuel Bretón de los Herreros, to show how greatly satisfied he is with the portrayal of Don Frutos in his wonderful comedy, *The Country Bumpkin,* has offered me the original manuscript of the play. You can imagine how flattered I am by this unique distinction."[34]

Lombía could not have known that he had just performed the most outstanding role in all of Bretón's theater. *Die and You Will See!* may be his best play and *Marcela* the universal favorite, but the part of Don Frutos in *The Country Bumpkin* is the best known in Bretonian repertory. Representing one of the two poles of Spanish humor, the rustic from the north, he is not unlike the provincial characters of other countries, for example, the American frontiersman of motion picture fame.

Frutos is much taller than most men: "he has a good figure / and the height of a grenadier." (Act I, scene i). He is also as strong as an ox: one day in Cariñena[35] he carried "four *quintales* of rice."[36] Like Don Pablo of *Die and You Will See!,* Frutos is blond and fair and consequently pleasing to women; one can see him towering over his rival, another northerner, the swarthy, tough, jealous, quarrelsome Captain Miguel, who challenges him to a duel. Frutos is to choose weapons, and like Little John in *Robin Hood,* names the cudgel! Miguel is aghast at his choice of arms.

Bretón carefully constructs the character of Frutos by scores of suggestions in the spectacle and dialogue of this play. The brusque Aragonese takes out an otterskin pouch and extracts a cigar, which he smokes in front of the ladies: this was unheard of in Madrid society. His appearance is such that "he looks as if he has come to sell melons." On another occasion, the marquesa, his future mother-in-law, archly observes that he has the "toilette of a coachdriver." The gloves they give him burst on his hands, and the foppish under-sized boots which he must wear *de rigueur* pinch his feet.[37] His necktie chokes him, and finally, in desperation, he doffs his Madrid wardrobe and puts on a sheepskin coat.

The dialogue supports the spectacle of a twenty-five year old country boy in the foppish atmosphere of Madrid. When Frutos comes to Elisa's house, he addresses the maid and embraces her, thinking she is to be his fiancée. When he sees a girl, he says: "Adiós, cordera" ("Hello, lamb."). Advised that "God keep you" is an uncouth greeting and that one must kiss the ladies' feet, he verbally asks Elisa and her mother for all four feet; he is sure he has counted well ("La cuenta no marra"). When he receives his new city jacket and is told not to button it, for such is the fashion of Madrid, he makes the classic reply: "What are the buttonholes for?" Finally, in spite of his dislike for city ways, he will go through with the marriage to Elisa, a marquesa's daughter:

FRUTOS:	when the girl's so pretty
	who pays me such an honor,
	I can well resign myself,
	sinner that I am, to being a marquis.
ELISA:	Did you hear, Mama? He resigns himself!
MARQUESA:	Eh! Don't take it as an insult.
	He's not too sharp with words. (Act II, scene iii)

Although Frutos cuts a ridiculous figure, he is never a mere clown or puppet but an intelligent observer of the environment who makes discerning remarks about the city: through his words and actions the reader learns what Madrid with its coxcombs was like.

As a good Aragonese, Frutos must keep his word: "Not even an earthquake. / I have never broken my word, / never! I am Aragonese." (Act IV, scene viii). Consequently he will go through with the marriage his father has promised, although he prefers not to. It is not to be supposed, however, that he cannot please a girl like Elisa; in Act II, scene xi, he recites some memorable lines, ending: "you will teach me how to speak, / and I will teach you how to love." (Act II, scene xi). Don Frutos is a man of noble bearing, but he is like a fish out of water in the Madrid of beaus and dandys. Although his awkwardness is an object of fun, the laughter is external; he is still a man of good stature whom any girl might marry.

Several speeches of *The Country Bumpkin* give the reader an insight into nineteenth century society. Frutos's relation with Elisa is typical of the marriages of convenience of that day;[38] he is wealthy but without a title, and she a titled woman without wealth. On seeing Frutos's rusticity, his greedy future mother-in-law exclaims:

> What a conflict, eternal God!
> What an outrage, most Holy Virgin!
> That I accept as son-in-law
> a Frutos Calamocha![39]
> But if I unite my line with his,
> who will bear me reproach?
> What role is there in the world
> for a marquesa without a coach?
> The wedding doesn't exactly please me,
> but this century's so businesslike....
> I see that hard cash money
> is also an aristocracy.   (Act I, scene iii)

Later in the play, when the marquesa tries to convince her daughter that Frutos can be domesticated, she leaves an indelible portrait of frivolous Madrid society (Act II, scene i). Other memorable passages are those on wives and husbands (the Marquesa, Act II, scene i), on clothes (Frutos, Act II, scene iii), and the *redondillas* of Elisa and Frutos in Act IV, scene viii. A particularly humorous character is the fence-sitter, Don Remigio, who, threatened by Miguel, attempts to disrupt the wedding of Frutos and Elisa.

VII   *The* "Comedia de Figurón"

The Country Bumpkin has been called a *comedia de figurón,* "a comedy in whose protagonist is portrayed some ridiculous and extravagant characteristic or vice,"[40] in the tradition of Rojas Zorrilla's play *Entre bobos anda el juego* (1638).[41] There are many likenesses between the two plays: both have a principal character who cuts a foolish appearance; both have a parent forcing a daughter into a marriage of convenience; both contain prominent speeches criticizing husbands as bad (Rojas) or stupid (Bretón); Rojas's play has an overturned horse coach bringing the characters together, and Bretón's sequel to *The Country Bumpkin, Don Frutos en Belchite* Don Frutos in Belchite, 1845, has the same accident; Bretón's Don Frutos (fruits) bears an odd name similar to Rojas's Don Lucas del Cigarral (fruit garden, or orchard); and in both plays a young girl must choose between two or three suitors. *Entre bobos* also has a traditional figure of fun, the humorous servant Cabellera, to support the humor, and Bretón has the family factotum, Remigio, a cowardly fence-sitter, carry out the same function. When creating *The Country Bumpkin,* Bretón had the example of Rojas's *comedia* before him.

The dissimilarities between a seventeenth century play (1638) and a nineteenth century play (1840), however, are also very great. Bretón writes "a la pata la llana,"[42] plainly and unaffectedly; his play is far more simple both in plot and versification than Rojas Zorrilla's. *The Country Bumpkin* has one love story, Elisa's, in which Frutos must contend with one visible rival, Miguel, whereas *Entre bobos* has all the intrigue of a *comedia de capa y espada:* several characters talk to one another in the dark, mistaking their interlocutors for other persons; until the last pages of the play Bretón's characters speak plain, unadorned words of love, whereas Rojas's speak in a labyrinthine way.[43] Still another difference between *Entre bobos* and *The Country Bumpkin* comes to mind. In the Spanish theater, Rojas's Don Lucas was the first of the old men who wanted to marry a young girl against her will,[44] and he was a fool (*necio*). But the twenty-five year old Frutos is no fool ("Pues no es tonto, aunque grosero" — Act I, scene x), and his ridiculousness is external, coming from the juxtaposition of rural and urban ways. He so captivated the Madrid audiences that they wanted to see him marry Elisa, and thus, five years later, Bretón produced a sequel, *Don Frutos in Belchite.*[45]

VIII Don Frutos in Belchite (Don Frutos en Belchite, *1845*)

In the second play the tables are turned: Elisa comes to Belchite rather than Frutos to Madrid, and the latter is no longer the Aragonese hayseed:

Don Frutos has given up his villager's garb, and he is
no longer so gruff in his speech or brusque in his
manner. (Stage directions: Act I, scene viii)

My inspection clearly shows
Don Frutos is another man.   (Act II, scene i)

Don Frutos is embarrassed by the awkwardness of other villagers, especially the greedy Tío Pablo and his daughter, Simona, who wants to marry Frutos, and with this embarrassment there vanishes the splendid, ingenuous character of the country bumpkin. The ending of the play, when Frutos and Elisa announce their engagement, foreshadows the lachrymose drama of later playwrights.

Notwithstanding its limitations, *Don Frutos in Belchite* has several highlights: the colorful speech of Tío Pablo and Simona,[46] and the *jota* scene of Act I; the dialogue of Frutos and Elisa in Act II, scene ii; and the figure of the notary, Mamerto, who manages to weep in Belchite! (Act I, scene v).[47]

IX The Ferry-Girl From Pasajes (La batelera de Pasajes, *1842*)

In one of his *Satires,* "La Manía de Viajar,"[48] Bretón comments on the new rage of many Spaniards:

> And fashion, in faith, has many strange quirks!
> What would the parents of my grandfather say
> If they returned to the world today?
> ....
> Today we are engaged in the opposite abuse.
> The Spaniard who travels not now is defamed.
> Nobody is content where God has put him.

In these verses Bertón is playfully chiding his friend, the Marqués de Molíns, who travels about so much that he always keeps one step ahead of his letters, in Paris, Leghorn, Alicante, Madrid, Geneva, Baeza, and other cities. Bretón's tercets, written in 1845, reveal the profound change taking place in Spanish society. The traditionally sedentary Spaniard was traveling all over the provinces and continent.[49]

After the termination of the Carlist civil war in 1839, Bretón, along with many other Madrilenians, began to travel to the Basque seacoast for his vacation.[50] There he visited the town of Pasajes, where the traveler needed an open boat, known as a *batel,* to get from one point of land to another. The rowers of these boats were the famous boatwomen (*bateleras*) of Pasajes, who have been described by one traveler in this way:

Some fifty women, arranged in a single line like a company of infantry, seemed to be waiting for someone and to be calling him and claiming him with tremendous screaming. The thing astonished me very much, but what doubled my surprise was the realization after a minute or so that the one

Three Major Plays

they were waiting for, calling by name, and claiming, was me.... They were calling me in the most expressive and diverse patomimes and not one of them advanced toward me. They looked like living statues rooted in the ground, to whom some magician had said: Shout all you want, gesture all you want, but do not move a step.... The population of this town has only one industry: working on the water. The two sexes have divided this work according to their strength. The men to the ships, the women to the inlet; the men go out fishing and leave the bay, the women stay in the bay and "pass over" all those whose business or interests lead them to San Sebastian. Hence, these boatwomen [*bateleras*]. These poor women have a passenger so infrequently that it was absolutely necessary for them to have an understanding. Otherwise, at the advent of each passer-by, they would have devoured each other and perhaps the passer-by himself. They have established a limit they do not go beyond and a policy they do not violate. It is an extraordinary country.[51]

This paragraph from Victor Hugo is rather like a paraphrase of the finest passage in all Bretón's theater, the first act of *The Ferry-Girl From Pasajes*.

A   Act I

The stage represents the inlet of the port of Pasajes, at a place known as La Herrera, on the road to San Sebastián. It is daybreak, an important consideration, since the director can stage the opening scenes in semidarkness, until the captain enters in scene iii; the lighting can then be increased, making him emerge as it were from the darkness, fulfilling Faustina's dream.

Faustina, the beautiful, barefooted girl of Pasajes, she of the white foot, golden hair, and graceful form ("Con esa rubia trenza / sobre el airoso talle" — Act I, scene iv), is hitching her boat to a rock and talking to her friend, Petra. The latter has slept well, but not Faustina, who has had a reverie in which a gallant man, a captain, has asked her to be his wife. His vague image resides in her fancy (*magín*), and she wonders if she will ever meet him. She is disturbed. Petra tells her that she had better lower her desires to a corporal or a sergeant or to a fine lad like Pablo, the fisherman of Lezo who has enlisted in the army. But Faustina replies: "Quiero querer, lo confieso, / mas no sé cómo ni a quién!" ("I want to love, I confess, / but I don't know how or whom"). She is twenty years old, not the fourteen year old girl she was when Pablo went away, and she carries a captain's image in her soul.[52]

A song is heard offstage, and in scene ii, the prows of several boats appear, each guided by a boatwoman of Pasajes. They sing their chorus: "Quickly, come quickly / for the sea is calm / ¡laralá!" Some of them approach Faustina and argue with her, out of jealousy, but then a passenger is seen and they line up and start calling him, in the very way Victor Hugo described. We learn why not one of them will put a foot forward:

FIRST BATELERA: And the girl who puts one foot forward
will buy, you know full well,
cider for all.

The passenger is Captain Bureba, whose eyes fall on Faustina:

¿Por qué así tan retirada, bella barquera? . . . . Tú has de ser mi batelera, ya que me dan a escoger.	Why so withdrawn, beautiful boat-girl? . . . . You are to be my boat-girl, since they have given me a choice.

The other *bateleras* leave the scene to provide transportation for the townspeople.

In the last scene of Act I, Bureba woos Faustina with the language of an educated man. And he is extremely handsome in his uniform.

¡Bien haya una y mil veces la playa de La Herrera que cría entre sus peces tan linda batelera! . . . . Con esa rubia trenza sobre el airoso talle y el sombrerillo leve, que amor formarlo pudo, y albo como la nieve el bello pie desnudo. . . . . ¡Y quién no lo[53] sería luego que te mirara? Que hay mucha poesía en tu donosa cara.	Praised be a thousand times the beach of La Herrera, which has raised amongst its sealife such a beautiful *batelera!* . . . . With those golden braids above that graceful waist, and the little bonnet, which love might have woven, and the beautiful bare foot as white as the snow. . . . . And who would not be a poet the moment he looked on you? For much is poetry in your pretty face. . . . .

Three Major Plays

Y pongo por testigo	And I invoke heaven
al cielo, ¡oh mi tesoro!	as my witness, oh my treasure!
que la verdad te digo	that I speak to you the truth
si digo que te adoro.	when I say I adore you.
. . . .	. . . .
Sí, batelera mía,	Yes, my *batelera,*
y si el amor te humana,	and if love softens your heart,
bien puede ser que un día	you may very well one day be
tú seas capitana.	a captain's only bride.
. . . .	. . . .
¡Tan bella criatura	Such a beautiful creature
remar cual galeote!	rowing like a slave!
. . . .	. . . .
¡Faustina! Yo te adoro.	Faustina! I adore you.

The young girl is confused, and between each of the captain's verses she struggles to free herself from the spell:

Eh, ¡señor!, no comience	Oh, sir!, don't start
a usar esos . . . lenguajes.	to use those big words
Más claro es el vascuence	Far clearer is the Basque
que hablamos en Pasajes.	we speak here in Pasajes.

She tells him the local teacher is a poet and that he lies to beat the band ("miente que se las pela"). She tells the captain his words are not believable ("Esa no cuela"). When he goes to touch her, she flashes back: "Easy! I am no guitar!" But little by little she falls within his net,[54] and finally can do no more than repeat a feeble *estribillo,* to delay the crisis: "Vamos a Pasajes / a ver al comodoro" ("Let us go to Pasajes / to see the commodore").[55] In the very last line of Act I, she rows with her right hand, places her left index finger across her lips, and says: "¡Chit! ... Boga, Petra, y vamos/a ver al comodoro!" ("Shh! Row, Petra, and let's go/to see the commodore"). All the boatwomen appear in the background, repeating their chorus — Curtain. We do not know Faustina's destiny in any scientific manner, but we can divine it. The gallant captain with his overpowering words has conformed to the image in her fantasy. His *tulle* responds to her ideal, and she will be his.

The singular charm of Act I, which lies in its fragmentary nature, resembles the ancient ballads of Spain. Of these ballads Menéndez Pidal has said:

But on going through an old *Romancero* [*Ballad Book*] of the sixteenth

century, we are surprised by the great abundance of unfinished events....
The Infante Arnaldos, which all admire as the principal masterpiece of the *Romancero,* as an archetype of ballads, is nothing else than a fragmentary version; here the abrupt ending transformed a simple ballad of adventures into a ballad of fantastic mystery, and this did not come about by chance, but rather after several trials at a final truncation, some of which are preserved for us in the old song books. The special touch of the abrupt cutting-off thus appears as a true poetic creation.

The *fragmentarism* of the *Romancero* is then an aesthetic procedure: fantasy leads a dramatic situation to its culminating point, and there, at the top, it flutters toward an unknown beyond, without descending on the slope of denouement.[56]

Act I of *La batelera* displays the same fragmentary art as the famous *romance morisco* (Moorish ballad), "La Mora Moraima":

Yo me era mora Moraima,	There I was the Moorish girl Moraima,
morilla de un bel catar;	Moorish lass with a pretty face;
cristiano vino a mi puerta,	the Christian came to my door,
cuitada por me engañar.	anguishing to deceive me.

The deceitful Christian convinces Moraima with his words, and at the end she opens the door for him:

vistiérame una almejía,	I put on a short cloak,
no hallando mi brial,	not finding my rich silken skirt,
fuérame para la puerta	I went to the door
y abríla de par en par.	and I opened it wide.

Moraima's short cloak will reveal her corporal beauty, in the same way Faustina's bare feet reveal hers. And the last line, "abríla de par en par," leaves the listener in suspense, in the same fashion as Faustina's "vamos a ver al comodoro." We the listeners know and yet we do not know. Both poem and play, in Menéndez Pidal's words, "flutter toward an unknown beyond."

B *Acts II, III, IV*

Act I is a fragment, rather like an episode from the *Romancero.* Proof of its fragmentary nature can be seen in Acts II, III, and IV, which are really a three act play separate from the bay scene at Pasajes.[57] Although they constitute a rather interesting play, they do not meet the standards of Act I.[58]

Three Major Plays 99

The setting has changed. Here are Bretón's stage directions:

Act II: The theater represents in this and the remaining acts the interior of a military tent, which serves as a camp canteen. A table in the background with bottles, flasks, food, cigars, etc. The door leading out to the field is to the right of the actor: to the left is another leading to a dormitory and further upstage is a portable stove: on both sides are canvas chairs.

Thus the setting of the last three acts is much more confining than the bay scene at Pasajes; indeed, it has basically the same dimensions as the Madrid drawingroom of so many other Bretonian plays.

The characters of the last three acts have also been changed, except for Faustina and Captain Bureba. Gone are Petra, the boatwomen, and the townsfolk, who have been replaced by the sergeants Pablo and Briones; by an adjutant, a chaplain, a surgeon; and by a supporting cast of soldiers. The poetic suggestion of Act I is followed now by the logical consequences of an honorable woman's being wronged by a lustful captain.

In camp after camp, Faustina has looked for Bureba, who had given her a false name. She comes now to the canteen of Sergeant Briones, Pablo's close friend. She sees Pablo for the first time in five and a half years and tells him of her fate: she wants to restore her honor. It turns out that Pablo's valiant captain is none other than Bureba, who offers Faustina money and then runs off when the call to arms is sounded.[59] Bureba is gravely wounded and marries Faustina, supposedly on his deathbed. But he recovers, with the result that Pablo and Faustina, who now loves this "fisherman of Lezo," are separated. In the lachrymose final scenes, Bureba is killed in a duel, and the young couple will marry "after the required period of mourning."

The redeeming features of Acts II, III, and IV are the character of Sergeant Briones and Bretón's deep knowledge of military life. Briones, whose name (*brío-brión*) suggests vigor and courage, is an outgoing, big-hearted, talkative buck sergeant who fancies he has a way with the ladies. He speaks the language of the common soldier: *drecho, camela, ensinia, estampía, cencia, caliá, leición, abriguar, mequinencias.* When the captain is gravely wounded, Briones is apt to say: "¿Se naja, según eso...?" (*Najarse* in slang means "to get out," or "to leave"); or perhaps: "Lía el petate / cualquier día" ("He's packing it in, / any day now"). When his wife deserts him for a supply officer, he calls Faustina: "El ama ha tomado la pipa" ("The canteen boss has flown the coop"). And the reader learns something about military graft in Bretón's day:

> BRIONES: It produced at least
> seven *pesetas* each day.
> But who can compete
> with a comissary officer?
> ....
> Isn't that man content
> with clipping off
> our biscuit and our bacon?   (Act II, scene ii)

The comissary officer not only clips off the bacon and biscuit of a soldier; he also clips off his wife.

Briones also speaks of the food in his canteen: *sagardúa, chacolí, aguardiente de guindas, un par de sardinas.*[60] He draws on card games for his imagery ("¡Buen julepe habéis llevado, / Carlistas!") And who but he, trying to encourage his young friend Pablo would think of a punning proverb like this:

Ten pecho y criarás espalda.	(Literally): Have a chest and you will grow a spine.
	(Figuratively): Take heart and you'll see it through.

X   La batelera: *Comedy or Drama?*

The Ferry-Girl From Pasajes gave rise to a critical debate: was it a comedy or a drama? One reviewer asked: "Why does the poet, who has called *Die and You Will See!* a comedy, call the *Ferry-Girl* a drama, like his *Elena*?" Another reviewer made a firmer judgement concerning the issue: "As to whether the play is a drama or not, we reply in the negative; but this matters little to us, because the fact is that its characters are well portrayed, and it is the production the author has most enriched with his customary comic wit."[61] The question of *comedy* or *drama* was still unsettled a half century later. In his chapter on Bretón, Piñeyro (1904) says it is a work of "hybrid character,"[62] whereas Blanco García, writing in 1909, called it a drama.[63] Bretón himself wrote a footnote about this question for the posthumous edition of his works in 1883. It is reproduced here, since it throws further light on the nature of Bretonian theater:

When I gave this composition to the theater, and also when ... I reprinted it in 1850, I classified it as a *drama*. Every *comedy* is a *drama;* everybody knows this; but in modern times the term *drama* is preferred when the pathetic, the terrible, and the extraordinary takes precedence over that which, in a festive and epigrammatic tone, portrays ordinary characters and customs, praising them or reprehending them. And *drama* is preferred when the action induces weeping rather than laughter. It seemed to me that *The Ferry-Girl From Pasajes* was such a work, because, after all, rather than comically develop the popular character of the protagonist I tried to show vividly the force and nobility of her soul in the various interesting situations which tested these qualities and also endangered her life and honor; it was a *drama* also because she redeemed her honor when Bureba married her *in articulo mortis;* and with Bureba's death she subsequently redeemed her own life and that of Pablo. Later, however, I thought that, since the outcome is happy for the two persons I hoped to make most likeable (although, given the plan I conceived, they couldn't be happy unless another less worthy person perish), and since more than half of the scenes belonged to the genre properly called comic, this dramatic production should be known as *comedia* and nothing else. (*Obras 1883*, III, 85)

Behind this argument one senses the broody side of nineteenth century thought. Somehow or other a comedy must be inferior to a drama, and it was thought to be unquestionably inferior to a tragedy. Comedies make people laugh and therefore lack the seriousness suitable for high-minded persons, whereas dramas, with "the pathetic, the terrible, the extraordinary," make people weep — and think! — and so they are better. It is unfortunate that Bretón had to make so many *distinguo's* in his apology for *The Ferry-Girl*. He seems to be saying: "I should like to call *The Ferry-Girl* a drama for various reasons, but they've got me marked down as Bretón the comediographer, the festive fellow, and so I shall have to call it a comedy after all. But please don't apply the word to every one of my plays, for I too can be high-minded."

We need not wonder at Bretón's apology for his theater, or at the humiliation he must have suffered. Nineteenth century French critics subjected even their prince of comediographers to the same treatment; as Brunetiére reminds us,

I know it is difficult to make oneself understood, and I willingly admit that whoever does not succeed has himself to blame. But really, with every allowance for my own incompetence, I would never have believed it would have been so hard to convince certain Frenchmen — dramatic authors, professors, journalists, and lecturers — that Molière would not be Molière had he not thought sometimes; that there is something more in him than a classic Labiche; and that after seeing *École des Femmes* or the *Malade imaginaire,* and laughing heartily at Arnolphe or the worthy Argan, we still carry away with us something to think over for a long time. For having dared to say so, indeed, I find that I am reminded on all sides of the false modesty which is expected of the commentator, and I would have been required to treat Molière as a merry-andrew or buffoon, in order not to cause alarm among those who will on no account allow their notion of him to be disturbed;...[64]

Criticized like Molière for writing comedies, an allegedly inferior genre, Bretón found himself in good company.

CHAPTER 8

Bretón and the Drama

WE have seen above that Bretón was often accused of superficiality. Don Juan Valera was speaking for most nineteenth century critics when he wrote:

It is true that the poet rarely penetrates the depths of the human soul. The great and vehement passions that are born in the soul are not usually the object of Bretón's study.

The love affairs, the domestic intrigues, the defects and extravagances, the whims of fashion, all of this, viewed superficially, served Bretón for plotting and planning his attractive, original comedies, which number more than a hundred.

Bretón limited himself to portraying what he most commonly saw: a middle class much more modest, much poorer, and enjoying fewer luxurious frills than today's... middle class, in brief,... *a la pata la llana.*[1]

Most of Bretón's plays were like his middle class, *a la pata la llana,* plain and unaffected. His contemporary critics were concerned about their ordinariness and longed for more adornment and some affectation. Bretón commented on the suasion, or dissuasion, of these critics in a footnote to *Elena,*[2] and their influence can be seen in the dozen or more dramas he wrote in order to please them. By urging Bretón toward "the poisonous pastry we call serious literature,"[3] they were diverting him from his real talent.

Bretón's dramas fall into several divisions: (*1*) *Elena,* 1834, which is *sui generis* a Romantic drama built on Bretón's "whom shall I marry" dilemma (it takes place in his own nineteenth century!); (*2*) the medieval dramas, *Don Fernando el Emplazado* (*Don Fernando the Summoned,* 1837), and *Vellido Dolfos,* 1839; (3) the dramas of the War of the Spanish Succession, *No ganamos para sustos* (*Never at Ease,* 1839), and *Estaba de Dios* (*What's To Be Is To Be,* 1842); (4) the Philip IV or Quevedo dramas, *¿Quién es ella?* (*Show Me the Woman,* 1849), and *Finezas contra desvíos*

(*Treat Disdain With Love,* 1843). There are also another half dozen plays that might be categorized as socio-novelistic-historical dramas;[4] it is significant that three of these dramas, *La independencia, La cabra tira al monte,* and *La niña del mostrador,* are the only full-length plays Bretón wrote in prose after 1825. They have been discussed in Chapter 4.

I *Romanticism and* Elena

The Spaniards of Bretón's day were puzzled by the appearance of Romanticism, and their reactions were ambivalent. Perhaps they sensed that the Romantic transition from intellect to will was a good thing; certainly some relaxation was in order. The stage itself had been hidebound by laws called *unities,* which were rather like three censors, while the new Romantic theater offered more liberty from rigid rules; on the other hand, there was something uncanny about all that Romantic defiance and suicide — Don Alvaro hurling himself off a cliff with Satanic grin, and in priestly garb! And the real-life suicide of Mariano José de Larra didn't help any; for Spanish Catholics, the impossibility of subsequent repentance made suicide especially horrific.

At the time, some changes of Romanticism were welcome, the variety, the beauty, the newness, the open door, the relaxation, the unburdening of the other side of the human spirit; but other changes were frightening too, the odd attire, the Merovingian locks, the sacrilegious attitude, the potential uncontrollability of the whole movement. The good in Romanticism was appetizing; the unknown, frightening. There were those who saw an intrinsic relation between Romanticism and Christianity, especially in art. The playwright Tamayo y Baus, for example, held that classical tragedy is based upon the doctrine of fate, by which man must follow an inexorable path; consequently the theater itself is inexorable, with unities, a foreseen outcome, and stringent requirements concerning the use of verse and prose. He held that Romanticism, with its unforeseen conclusion, its generosity with respect to laws, its mixture of verse and prose, its unpredictability, is completely free and thus consonant with — indeed, it is a result of — Christian free will. Paganism permits one form, fate; whereas Romanticism and Christianity permit as many forms as there are human beings.[5] Another position was that of Juan Donoso Cortés, who saw a propitious relation between Romanticism and Christianity.

Donoso, however, was far less dogmatic than Tamayo and took an eclectic position in art: "Then perfection consists in being Classic and Romantic at the same time...."[6]

There were also those who strove to arrest the tide of Romanticism, at least in literature, by parody. Anything can be held in check provided it can be reduced to laughter. The most famous of all Madrilenians, Ramón Mesonero Romanos, wrote a celebrated article called "Romanticism and the Romantics" (September 1837), much enjoyed then and still enjoyed today.[7] It includes the outline of a play, *She!!! And He!!!*, a "Natural, Romantic Drama, Emblematic, Sublime, Anonymous, Synonymous, Gloomy, and Spasmodic, Original, In Diverse Verses and Prose, in Six Acts and Fourteen Scenes; it takes place in the fourth century, lasting a hundred years, and its cast: the *wife* (all wives, all women), the *husband* (all husbands), a savage man (the lover), the doge of Venice, the tyrant of Syracuse, the archduchess of Austria, a spy, a hangman, the Quadruple Alliance, a chorus of Carmelite nuns, a talking spectre, four gravediggers, a retinue of troops, witches, gypsies, friars, and many others. The six acts are entitled "A Crime," "The Poison," "Too Late," "The Pantheon," "She!," and "He!"

Bretón's general attitude toward Romanticism is not too unlike Mesonero's; see, for example, his one act play *The Outline of a Drama*, (*El plan de un drama*, 1835), which he wrote in collaboration with Ventura de la Vega. Bretón and Vega themselves appear in the play as authors of a new Romantic drama, *The Conspiracy*, and when they speak of "Let all die!," "Extermination!," "Conspiracy!," and the like, they are overheard by local constables who take them to be Carlist conspirators. Then Bretón and Vega are apprehended by the law. Both playwrights treated Romanticism jocundly, as did Mesonero.[8]

As an artist, however, Bretón profited by the innovations of Romantic literature. The formal liberalization of his own theater coincides with the appearance of Romantic works in Spain: in 1824, he started out with his Moratinian *The Young Old Codger*, adhering strictly to Neoclassical rules, which he continued to follow in his next six plays. Then with *Marcela*, in 1831, he inaugurated a more liberal structure.

Bretón's Romantic effort, *Elena,* appeared before the more famous Romantic works of the Spanish stage. Here is a chronological diagram:

La conjuracón de Venecia	Martínez de la Rosa	April 23, 1834
Macías	Larra	September 24, 1834
Elena	Bretón	October 23, 1834
Don Alvaro	Rivas	1835
Los amantes de Teruel	Hartzenbusch	1837
El Trovador	García Gutiérrez	1837

Elena appeared in the same year as Espronceda's novel *Sancho Saldaña* and Larra's novel *El doncel de don Enrique el doliente,* and ten years before Gil y Carrasco's novel *El señor de Bembibre* (1844). Thus Bretón, a Moratinian and a parodist of Romanticism (in 1835!), gave long serious thought to Romantic drama from the very start. He was no casual observer.

II Elena

The play opens with these verses, spoken by Don Gerardo, Elena's uncle:

> No curb now remains to my passion;
> now I have shame over so much
> weakness; I grow tired
> of whining and beseeching....
> Elena must be my wife:
> I swear it: she will be.
> Oh most unhappy woman
> if she disdains my charity!   (Act I, scene i)

If the reader takes Don Gerardo literally, he is the gloomy man (like Sancho Saldaña, the *hombre tétrico*), the passionate man, the man who knows no law, the man of force (like Hernani, *je suis une force*) of the Romantics. But something is awry. Gerardo explains too much in these lines, he confesses to weakness and shame, fatigue, whining and begging, and he is concerned about the vice of ingratitude ("si es ingrata"). There are no gypsies or other townfolk to refer to Gerardo as a mysterious being, for the good reason that he is not mysterious. It is not fate that leads him on, but only his own erotic desire. He is a nineteenth century uncle who wants to wed his nineteenth century niece, who in turn loves a nineteenth century marquis. One rival in love mentions a duet by Bellini and an aria from *The Lady of the Lake* (Act II, scene iv), and the bandits of Act IV probably constitute the beginning of nineteenth century melodrama in Spain.[9]

The five act *Elena* is far and away the longest play Bretón ever wrote. Its construction resembles Espronceda's novel *Sancho Saldaña,* with a multitude of events piled up until the last chapter, wherein all loose ends are suddenly brought together and everyone given a destiny; and its inverisimilitude is hardly different. The Conde will marry Victorina, the foul Ginés meets a horrible death, Rejón the bandit-soldier is converted to righteousness, the evil uncle commits suicide, and the marquis will marry Elena. This establishment of order represents an ancient thirst in Spanish theater, but it is nevertheless lacking in verisimilitude in *Elena.*

In brief, *Elena* is an embryonic Bretonian *comedia* with enough Romantic trappings to be called a *drama.*

III Don Fernando The Summoned (Don Fernando el Emplazado, 1837) and Vellido Dolfos (1839)

Don Fernando The Summoned and *Vellido Dolfos* are the two plays in which Bretón made his most intense Romantic effort.[10] The historical drama was in vogue at the time, and he was anxious to try his poetical gifts (*numen*) in every genre, having just enjoyed a resounding success with his translation of Delavigne's *The Sons of Edward;*[11] he was influenced by the example of Victor Hugo,[12] and his close friend Roca de Togores (Molíns) had produced a *María de Molina* (July 1837);[13] and Bretón was stimulated by and perhaps envious of Rivas's *Don Alvaro,* García Gutiérrez's *El trovador,* and Hartzenbusch's *Los amantes de Teruel* — for many reasons he was anxious to write an outstanding Romantic drama.

A. Don Fernando The Summoned

A famous legend of Spanish history describes the events of August 1312, when the young King Ferdinand IV ordered the execution of two innocent men, D. Juan and D. Pedro Carvajal, whom he accused of murdering D. Juan Alfonso Benavides. The Carvajals protested their innocence, and when they saw justice denied them:

they appealed their sentence to the tribunal of God, summoning King Ferdinand there in thirty days. This is the reason D. Fernando IV has been called *The Summoned One*.... In fact, the king left for Alcaudete, and having become ill he returned to Jaén, where on Thursday, in September of 1312, he expired within twenty-four hours, the very day on which the thirty days summons of the Carvajal brothers was up....

Whether this was an accident or a punishment from heaven, the death of the three persons is a question no man dare discuss, for the judgments of God are inscrutable to all. It behooves us not to investigate them, but to bow our heads before them.[14]

As late as 1860, when Antonio Benavides, a member of the Royal Academy of History, published his *Memorias de D. Fernando IV de Castilla,* there were historians who still did not question the legend but accepted it. This acceptance is the very fiber of Bretón's play of the year 1837, *Don Fernando The Summoned.* There is a good deal of embellishment — for example, the love story of Pedro Carvajal and the murdered man's sister, Sancha; the priestly character of Juan Carvajal; the addition of a third proud Carvajal, Gonzalo, who insists on honor; the false witness, Peláez, and the true witness, Fortún — but the play is steeped in history as Bretón and his contemporaries conceived it.

One scene in which the Carvajals are executed by being hurled from a cliff, will appeal to most readers:

SANCHA:
¡Oh peña, peña de Martos!	Oh cliff, oh cliff of Martos!
Si el esposo que perdí,	If the husband I have lost,
víctima de atroz venganza	victim of atrocious vengeance
y de la envidia más vil,	and of envy most unclean,
aun yace a tu pie insepulto	still lies untombed at thy feet,
allí está mi mundo, allí.	there is my world, and only there.
. . . .	. . . .
¡Ay de mí,	Oh woe is me,
que en hora amarga nací!	on a bitter day was I born!

(Act IV, scene xi)

B. Vellido Dolfos

On his death in 1065, Ferdinand I broke with the tradition of Gothic kings by dividing his kingdom into three parts instead of leaving it all to his oldest heir, Don Sancho the Strong. Throughout the next seven years Sancho waged war successfully against his family, until his sister Doña Urraca led the rebellion of Zamora. After a long siege, the city was on the point of surrendering to Sancho's forces when, on October 7, 1072, a Zamoran knight, Vellido Adolfos, managed to infiltrate the royal camp and assassinate the king. Since the Cid himself was Sancho's vassal, these events have entered Spanish literature in the ballads (*romances*) of the Cid:

Sobre el muro de Zamora	On the wall of Zamora
vide un caballero erguido	I saw a knight stand high
al real de los castellanos	and to the camp of Castilla
decía con grande grito:	he gave a mighty cry:
— ¡Guarte, guarte, rey don Sancho,	— Take care, take care, Don Sancho,
etc., etc.	etc., etc.

Bretón's drama, *Vellido Dolfos,* sticks close to the narrative and spirit of the ballads, although he adds one embellishment, the love of the ordinary knight, Vellido Dolfos, for Doña Urraca, princess of the royal blood. This love, a peculiar *amor loco* since he does not aspire to carnal union, leads to Vellido Dolfos's madness and the murder of Sancho.

Bretón's frequent use of the verse forms known as *romances heroicos* and *octavas reales* in these historical dramas is apparently meant to give them an epic quality, that is to say, profundity (he had been accused of superficiality). In effect, they result in a ponderous style.[15]

IV *The War of the Spanish Succession:* Never at Ease, (No ganamos para sustos, *1839) and* What's To Be Is To Be (Estaba de Dios, *1843*)

An effort at the historical drama, *Never at Ease*[16] will show that Bretón's genius is basically comic. It begins with a rather dramatic action in the first act, turns to the action of a *comedia de capa y espada* in the second act (two men are hidden in a lady's room), and winds up in the third act with the *gracioso,* the clown figure, having a most prominent role. Don Félix will not permit his daughter Serafina to marry until the play's end, when her love for Don Juan wins out.

Bretón employs a specific historical event in this play to disguise a deus ex machina conclusion. The action takes place in December 1710, when Marshall von Stajremberg and General Stanhope[17] were leading the allied forces against the Bourbon king, Philip V. Stajremberg had been victorious in July, at Almenara, but now, in

December, their enemy, the Duke of Vendome, triumphs over them. The defeat of the allies takes place at the very moment in Bretón's play when an allied sergeant is turning over the *gracioso* and Don Juan for military imprisonment. They are, of course, liberated at once. Bretón uses history in this same redemptory fashion in *La Independencia,* when Riego's uprising of March 1820 saves Don Agustín from death at the hands of the absolutists.

As theatrical editor for *El Correo Literario y Mercantil,*[18] Bretón often reviewed plays by Scribe and his associates that involved snares, trickery, contrived plots about foreign lands or visitors, mistaken identities, sudden changes of fortune, inheritances, and citizens of the New World returning to the Old in order to redress the balance of things (see, e.g., his reviews of Scribe's *El tutor inglés* and *Los primeros amores,* in the *Obra dispersa,* pp. 56-59). His own *What's To Be Is To Be* is a mixture of such a Scribian play with a regular *comedia bretoniana,* in which young love is hampered until the final scene.

To make his plot more plausible, Bretón places his action in 1709, a reasonably far-off time when customs were different from those of the 1840s. A guardian (Don Tadeo) had more power then; two marriageable girls (Paula and Margarita) had more traditional ideas about matrimony; and the imposter count (Ambrosio Pérez) might be apprehended for conspiring against Philip V. This count is humorous with his similicadences and other contrived punning ("¡Oh primo! En vano reprimo.... ¿Es éste mi primo?")

What's To Be Is To Be, like most of Bretón's plays, is also a mine for the paremiologist.

V *The Philip IV Plays:* Treat Disdain With Love
   (Finezas contra desvíos, *1843*) *and*
   Show Me The Woman (¿Quién es ella?, *1849*)

Treat Disdain With Love is set in a country home (*quinta*) outside of Madrid. Doña Leonor has a false lover, Don Diego, who wants to marry her for "vile interest," and a devoted lover, Don Félix, who answers her indifference (*desvíos*) with kindness (*finezas*). Act I seems to be Bretonian and in nineteenth century style; one gathers that Leonor, who is "an orphan and young," will finally choose Félix rather than Diego.

In Act II, however, the name of Philip IV (1605-1665) is introduced, and in Act III this king of lustful memory appears in person, complicating the action. Thus Acts I and II are basically Bretonian comedy, whereas Acts III and IV resemble a *comedia de capa y espada*,[19] with Diego wounded in a duel and the king and Félix hidden in Leonor's house. In *Treat Disdain With Love* Bretón was trying to please both his audiences, who wanted history, and his critics, who were accusing him of superficiality. The duenna, Doña Mencía, resembles the Spanish bawd and procuress, Celestina (see Act IV, scene v), and Don Diego is twice referred to as a *lindo don Diego* (conceited coxcomb), an obvious reference to Agustín Moreto's seventeenth century play, *El lindo don Diego*.

Show Me The Woman, the most famous of the plays Bretón set in an earlier century, figures among the four works Menéndez Pelayo ranked as "plays of exceptional quality." It places on the stage Don Francisco de Quevedo (1580-1645), the Juvenal of Spanish letters.[20] In a long footnote to the 1883 edition of *Show Me The Woman,* Bretón explains that he kept a "rigorous *incognito*" until the day after its première, his only confidantes being two close friends, Juan Eugenio Hartzenbusch and Ventura de la Vega. He himself did not do this "for the puerile reason of showing off," nor for "lending an air of importance to his work by making it seem mysterious, covering it with a veil." He wanted the work to be judged on its own merits, rather than on his name or reputation. He refers to certain habits of the press, by which a play is greeted with "inopportune praise which, rather than favor him, puts him in a difficult position," or with "censure showing little love for one's neighbor." Here Bretón was obviously concerned about "his cruelly bent and systematic enemies." He wanted to know what *Show Me The Woman* might intrinsically be worth: hence the incognito.[21]

Bretón then says that prior to the opening night of *Show Me the Woman,* while the incognito still prevailed, there were several official and private readings of "this foundling child of Thalia." The readers attributed the play to all the illustrious figures of "the contemporary Spanish Parnassus" except its own true father (Bretón himself). Some saw Bretón's hand in a certain scene, or in one *letrilla* or *quintilla* or another, "...but this interesting situation, these philosophically tender hendecasyllables ... cannot be the fruit of his pen, here is the hand of $H.....$; — this dialogue, conceptual and incisive, obviously belongs to $R.....$; and in more than one characteristic, in more than one episode, to whom is hidden the style of $V.....$, his good taste and his dramatic touch?"[22]

(*Obras 1883,* IV, 152) The readers were willing to assign Bretón "paternity" of certain parts of the play, the less serious ones, but they assigned the "paternity" of more lofty scenes to other authors. Bretón continues:

but when he saw the paternity of other scenes denied to him, he [Bretón] had to restrain himself violently so as not to protest against such a decision, and he had to remember that in his long career he believed he had demonstrated one truth: namely, that if in general, as a comic poet, he had preferred to make people laugh, other springs of the human heart were not unknown to him. He had also at times not unfruitfully tried to speak to the soul and imagination of the spectators, without using jocular dialogue. He had not for the first time in *Show Me the Woman* employed the discreet language of love but had used it often before, even throughout entire plays. This was not the first time he was putting his talents to the test in several areas, be it the sentimental, the picturesque, the pathetic, or even the terrible. And finally he [Bretón] might well be the *one and only author* of *Show Me the Woman,* in spite of the variety of tones its plot encouraged. (*Obras 1883,* IV, 153)

This long footnote[23] tells us a great deal about Bretón himself. He refers to himself in the third person in order to avoid the *yo, yo, yo* of an egotist, but the third person is even stronger than the first, rather like a third person *yoísmo.*[24] His constant use of negatives and double negatives in the note casts a mood of self-concern over the entire passage. Instead of saying "Others were named the father, I was not named the father," he seems to be saying: "There was nobody who was neglected as parent of this play except me; I was neglected even though many things were not unknown to me and indeed I knew them better than anybody else at the time." Curiously, Bretón's statement in the footnote is both subjectively and objectively true. He was old and bitter and felt hurt when he wrote it, and in truth many critics had been unjust with him, urging him to abandon his *vis cómica* as if its fruits were superficial.[25]

In the second act of *Show Me The Woman,* the misogynist Quevedo composes a *letrilla* on women:

> They tell the story about a magistrate,
>   no fool,
> that whene'er the good man was informed
> of murder or theft,
> he cut short the notary
> who read the complaint,

Bretón and the Drama

>saying: Let's get down to brass tacks, brass tacks!
>*Show Me The Woman.* (Act II, scene i)

But in the fifth act, having seen the heroic action of the countess and the virtue of the beautiful Isabel, this ferocious satirist must "sing the palinode," as Spaniards usually say:

>I bow before the evidence
>and base my case on justice.
>WOMAN is, I swear by Pindus,
>the most pleasant, the most pretty thing
>that God has placed in the world. (Act V, scene v)

Quevedo is joined by King Philip IV, who must sing the palinode in his own way. The most lascivious of monarchs, he is duty-bound to keep hands off Isabel, one of the court *meninas,* and to free her true love, Gonzalo, from jail. Philip's role in *Show Me The Woman* is rather like Segismundo's in *Life Is a Dream:* at first an apostle of discord, he becomes a justice-bearing king. Of all Bretón's historical plays, this is unquestionably the best.

CHAPTER 9

The Comediejas

I *Introduction*

ON February 9, 1838, Bretón wrote a letter to his friend, Mariano Roca de Togores (the Marqués de Molíns), saying: "Now I am given to writing *comediejas* in one or at most two acts.... It is true indeed that only by doing so am I able to please the actresses, who constantly make demands on my fancy for their benefit performances."[1] Spanish has more latitude than English in the formation of diminutives, augmentatives, and depreciatives. The depreciative suffix, *-eja,* on *comedia,* forming *comedieja,* suggests that Bretón is given to writing one act moneymakers, potboilers, grade B plays, the kind everyone will attend for a night's fun and soon forget. Bretón's judgement of his one act plays, which he also called *fabulillas, juguetes, sainetillos, dramitas, poemitas,* and *pasatiempos,*[2] is unreliable. He made such self-effacing remarks at the time he was under attack for superficiality by critics stressing the *utile* in the theater;[3] unless a comedy was dramatic with a serious lesson to it, they were not disposed to accept it. Some of Bretón's *comediejas* are in truth literary gems, like a short story by Pardo Bazán, a *leyenda* by Zorrilla, or an *entremés* from earlier centuries.

Bretón wrote thirty original *comediejas* and translated twenty-seven more from the French,[4] so he was thoroughly at home in the genre. Most of the original plots are set in Madrid, and most of them, like his full-length comedies, are written in verse.[5] The *comediejas* fall into several categories:

1. *Comedias de figurón: The Fat Man (El hombre gordo,* 1835). One act, in prose.
2. Situation comedies: *One More Coquette (Una de tantas,* 1837). One act, in verse.

3. Comedies about family problems: *Extraordinary Means* (*Medidas extraordinarias,* 1837). One act, in verse.
4. Satirical comedies: *The Peaceful Man* (*El hombre pacífico,* 1838). One act, in verse.
5. Topical comedies: *Phrenology and Hypnotism* (*Frenología y magnetismo,* 1845). One act, in verse.
6. Comedies of extreme contrivance (or "Sardoodledum"): *The Three Bouquets* (*Los tres ramilletes,* 1850). One act, in verse.
7. Comedies about the love of a man and woman: *Between A Saintly Man and Woman* (*Entre Santa y Santo,* 1862). One act, in prose.
8. Serious plays: *The Trials of Matrimony* (*Pruebas de amor conyugal,* 1840). Two acts, in verse.

These categories, which are not rigid and may overlap, will suggest the essential character of Bretón's *comediejas.* Let us now describe four of them.

II The Fat Man

The scene is set in Madrid in 1834 in the ticket office of a stagecoach company, about half an hour before the departure of the eleven o'clock coach. This modern concept of precise time is significant, for two young newlyweds, Luis and Rosita, are trying to escape from the latter's guardian, Don Jerónimo. A sense of haste prevails until the bells sound eleven o'clock, at the end.

The Fat Man has more characters (thirteen) than the usual five or six of a full-length Bretonian *comedia,* and since all of them crowd eventually into the ticket office and stagecoach, where they are talking back and forth and making fun of the fat man, the play is far more animated than most.

The fat man, that "calamity," that "obesity so outrageous and absurd," "that stupendous bulk, frightful individual, nonsensical abdomen, scandalous corpulence, and horrid pleonasm of the flesh," is Don Jerónimo, Rosita's uncle and guardian. Luis enlists the services of three students and a prankster friend (*calavera*), Esteban, to make sure the fat man does not get a seat on the stagecoach. War on all uncles and guardians, the enemies of the young! The youthful allies simply make sure the obese uncle does not get two adjoining seats, which his "pleonasm of flesh" requires. He has one ticket marked *interior* and another marked *berlin,* but they do him no good for his great self ("what a nefarious rump!") cannot be divided! The coach must leave without him. Young love is victorious, and the huge, immense, unmeasured *figurón,* figure of authority, is left in utter ridicule![6]

The Fat Man has many interesting sidelights: for example, the historically accurate need of passports for trips beyond six leagues from Madrid; the old couple, Don Venancio and Quiteria, whose affected manners date back to the eighteenth century; and the attempts of the students to Latinize everything. One aspect of the play merits study by future scholars, namely, its relation to French *vaudeville* (which should not be confused with the American variety show of the same name). Interspersed among the prose dialogues of the characters are verses, *redondillas* and *quintillas,* which are meant to be recited or sung;[7] for example, in one scene Don Jerónimo is humorously describing his own obesity: "I don't fit on any sidewalk; everyone bumps into me; ... People stop and stare at me and there's always one who laughs in my face. — 'When are they raffling you off?' — a fruit-seller said to me yesterday. Not a soul will rent me a *calesa.* I needed half a bolt of cloth to make this jacket, and, in short ..." Then he suddenly breaks out into verse:

> ...and in short
> there isn't a hat to fit me,
> not a chair where I can sit,
> nor a floor to hold me,
> nor a shoe that doesn't burst,
> nor an inn to feed me.   (Scene iv)

The Fat Man portrays some customs of the day and provides an evening of fun in the theater.

III   One More Coquette

The Spanish have an expression, *pelar la pava,* referring to the amorous talks young men and women have, the men from the street, the women from a grilled window or balcony. This was the traditional way of courting a girl in Spain.

Bretón's *One More Coquette*[8] might also have been called *Pelar la pava*[9] ("the flirtation"), a most unique flirtation in the theater. The Sevillian girl, Camila, has a house with two prominent sides, one facing the audience, the other facing stage right, both of them with grilled windows. It is 2:00 A.M. Lieutenant Miguel comes to

The Comediejas

one window, Captain Andrés to the other, and the "archcoquette," the "deceiver," the "jingle bell" Camila goes now to one window now to the other to flirt with both men alternately, giving a sick mother as her reason for absenting herself. From Andrés she accepts a ring and a lock, which she gives as keepsakes to Miguel, and from the latter she accepts a miniature portrait, which she immediately bestows upon Andrés. She swears undying love to both officers.

The night wears on and day breaks as Camila takes leave of the windows. The two men meet and talk of their courtships. Little by little they learn of their common folly:

MIGUEL:	Casa con dos puertas siempre fue mala de guardar.	A two-doored house was always hard to police. (An allusion to Calderón's play, *Casa con dos puertas mala es de guardar.*)
ANDRÉS:	Es a moza es de la piel del diablo, y dice el refrán: quien hace un cesto hará cien.	That girl is of the devil's hide and the proverb reads: he who steals a penny will steal a pound.

Both men abandon Camila, but she has another suitor waiting for her at early Mass, in the cathedral!

IV Phrenology and Hypnotism

In 1826, Henry David Inglis published *A Lecture Upon The Truth, Reasonableness and Utility of the Doctrines of Phrenology,* in which he said: "It is not intended in this lecture to do greatly more than to show that the doctrines of phrenology *may* be founded in truth, and are not therefore the proper subject of ridicule." Inglis argued that phrenology was "looked upon by the mass of the world as the subject only of mirth," although the bulk of mankind was "altogether ignorant of the doctrines they assail.[10]

Inglis's attitude is essentially that of Bretón, who is not ridiculing phrenology and hypnotism as such but the charlatans who practice them. The young lover in the play, Don Manuel, shows a certain sympathy for these sciences, or at least a hands-off attitude, on two occasions. Bretón also wrote a footnote for the posthumous 1883 edition, distinguishing between the use and abuse of a science.[11]

Bretón's *Phrenology and Hypnotism,* a topical comedy, is also a *comedia de figurón*. The humor, plot, and language of the play depend on the ridiculous appearance and actions of Don Lucas Pérez Orduña, the old phrenologist, who wants to marry the young widow, Luisa. Has anyone ever heard of a *redondilla* rhyming in consonance like this?:

Mas ya probaré en *detall*	But I shall prove in *detall* [detail]
que no es farsa ni pamema	that it's no farce or bunk
el admirable sistema	the admirable system
del famoso doctor *Gall*.	of the famous doctor *Gall*.
	(Scene iv)

Don Lucas is a spectacle in himself, dressed in elegant, old-fashioned clothes "of ridiculously loud colors, ill-matched." After feeling the heads of two candidates, he dismisses them as ineligible for a servant's job:

LUCAS:	Notice another advantage of the system of doctor *Gall*. To hire servants references are no longer needed. (Feeling his head.)
FIRST SERVANT:	What are you doing? (What a strange humor!)
(Trembling)	
LUCAS:	What a frightful development! What a mountain in the region of pride! Go away! Go away!
FIRST SERVANT:	Most holy Virgin! Why I'm as humble as a lamb and I hold a grudge against no man.

Lucas casts words about like protuberance, amativity, jokingness (*chistosidad*), craneoscopes, and acquisitive organ:

LUCAS:	His *acquisitive* organ is atrocious and in the ultimate state of malice and perversion....
CEFERINA:	Isn't it possible he have a bruise on that organ?

Lucas summarily dismisses the second candidate, (with the acquisitive organ), because he will surely be a thief. He then hires a servant whose head has "balanced organs," and the man steals his watch!

Lucas is most ridiculous as he gyrates around Luisa with an eyeglass to her head, trying to feel it, to see what sort of a wife she will be. He sees veneration standing out on her cranium: she will make a good spouse. At the end, Luisa submits to Lucas' hypnosis, which is his undoing. Feigning sleep, she says she will marry him, but calls him ugly and ridiculous. The wealthy old fool suspects her motives and will not marry her now. Young love wins out: Luisa will marry Manuel.

V Between a Saintly Man and Woman (Entre Santa y Santo): *An Ambulatory Comic Piece*

A Spanish proverb reads: "Entre santa y santo / pared de cal y canto" ("Between a saintly man and woman / a solid wall and strong"). It is dangerous for a man and woman, no matter how great their virtue, to be alone together.[12] This "eloquent proverb" suggested to Bretón the possibility of "an ambulatory comic piece."[13] His play, most of which takes place in the front compartment of a stagecoach, was designed for the reading public rather than the stage. The three main characters have inner thoughts that would require extreme adaptation for presentation in the theater. Thus, *Between a Saintly Man and Woman* is a *novella* or story-in-dialogue, similar in this respect to the *Celestina* or to Baroja's *Paradox, Rey.*

The plot is simple. The young widow (*viudita*) Doña Engracia, who is traveling in La Rioja with her maid and friend, Manuela, has reserved two of three seats in the compartment of a stagecoach. She mourns her dead husband and will become a nun; she has a low opinion of men. Manuela, on the other hand, has a great deal of common sense and recognizes the true promptings of nature. Don Modesto, a gentleman of "twenty-eight or thirty," takes the third seat in the dead of night, with a wine canteen at his side, a cigar in his mouth, and a basket filled with food. None of the characters can see the other two.

Modesto has been betrayed by a coquette he truly loved and now has a low opinion of women. He is polite and observes all the amenities, but "the daughters of Eve" cannot be trusted. However, Engracia and Modesto are closeted together in the small compartment, along with nature's advocate, Manuela. The charm of this "ambulatory comic piece" consists in the transition of Engracia and Modesto from cool traveling companions to two people, a *santa* and *santo,* deeply in love. Manuela tells Engracia:

y usted no tiene talle de monja.	and you don't have the figure of a nun.
Engracia: ¿Qué tiene que ver el talle con la ...	What has figure got to do with the...
Manuela: Con tocas y todo será usted siempre linda; convengo en ello.	With nun's coif and all you will still be pretty; I'm sure of that.
	(scene i)

Manuela also says: "Nature also has her prescriptions and they are most effective." (scene i)

The calm Modesto starts out thinking and talking like this: "No; I will confine myself to looking at women with philosophical and tranquil, but polite and benevolent indifference." (scene iii) Nonetheless, as dawn enters the compartment, throwing light on Engracia's face and form, he starts to change. He has been calling her *Señora,* and gradually changes to *Engracia, Engracita,* "sus dientes de aljófar," *hermosa Engracia;* and when he offers her food, everything goes into the diminutive: does she want some *lonjita, rebanadita, traguito, vasito, sorbito.* Then he uses the familiar *tú* with Manuela, though still calling Engracia *usted.*

Engracia is calling him *Don Modesto* now and thinks to herself: "Ah! I don't know what has come over me." She weeps and tells Manuela: "I am crying, I am so weak"; and finally she confesses: "I suspect that I, ay! .... that I love him!" Always discreet, but less discreet now in her discretion, she lets Manuela do much of her talking for her. And nature takes its course. In a storm, the travelers must abandon the coach and walk to a neighboring town. Engracia and Modesto share the same cape for protection against the elements. They will be husband and wife ere long. *Between a Saintly Man and Woman* is one of the finest pieces Bretón ever wrote, a small, forgotten classic. It seems ironic that Bretón, who prided himself on his three act comedies in verse, wrote this fine *novella* in prose.[14]

CHAPTER 10

Of Opuscules and Poetry: Tying Up Loose Ends

BRETÓN'S nondramatic works in prose consist of some thirty festive articles and *artículos de costumbres,* several hundred newspaper and review articles, an *Art of Declamation,* and the *Résumés of Acts and Deeds* he wrote as secretary of the Royal Academy.¹ All these works, which would fill several volumes, reveal the intense activity of a man who was simultaneously writing scores of original plays and translations for the stage.

I *The* Articles of Local Color (Artículos de Costumbres)

The collected *Obras* of 1850–1851 contained twenty-five articles, including those classified as "Spanish types," for example, "The Chestnut Vendor," "The Wet-Nurse," and "The Washerwoman." The *Obras* of 1883, retaining the three Spanish types, omitted the other articles but added three more "opuscules in prose" — "The Gambling Woman," "The Stone Marriage," and "The Sabbath." Le Gentil's important book in French, *Le Poète Manuel Bretón de los Herreros,* has an appendix with two additional *artículos de costumbres,* "The Masks," and "Courtship."²

What are these articles like? Molíns describes them in glowing terms: "But the place where his observant, nimble, and festive spirit is revealed, his liveliness and truth in the portrayal of characters, his richness and masterliness in handling the language, his *vis cómica* in short . . . is in the long series of *artículos de costumbres* he inserted in those newspapers."³ Le Gentil's judgement of the articles is less glowing; for him they are "amusing sketches" but they are also "banal analyses."⁴ A description of one article, "The Chestnut Vendor," will give a fair idea of Bretón's *costumbrismo.* In "The [Woman] Chestnut Vendor" ("La Castañera"), Bretón begins with a jestful popular etymology of the word *castaño* (chestnut tree), relating it to *casto* (chaste) and then wondering about the *castidad* (chastity) of the *castañera*. This kind of tasteless humor, easily achieved by a lesser talent, is rare in his works.

He then passes on to social commentary. The *castañera*, who goes far back in Spanish history and literature,[5] reached her apogee in the third part of the eighteenth century, but nowadays "our *castañeras* are not even a shadow of what they used to be." Why have the *castañeras* changed so radically? Bretón offers an explanation based on class:

What we call the lower class has declined in quality and quantity, just as the aristocracy has decayed in wealth and authority. The middle classes are visibly absorbing both extremes, a phenomenon owing in part to the progress of civilization, in part to the influence of political institutions, the advantages and disadvantages of which I do not propose to discuss. The fact is, one no longer gets a glimpse of those ruffians whose sinister mien must still be present in the memory of a certain famous person of the court of Charles IV,[6] nor does one see those Madrid gals [*manolas*] who blessed Murat's soldiers with a two pound weight when they dared to make love to them. (*Obras 1883*, V, 501)

Although Bretón tells his reader that times are changing, he does not display the extreme nostalgia of later writers such as Pereda and Palacio Valdés; he is no *laudator temporis acti*. On the other hand, he does not attain the poignancy of Larra in a similar article, "Modos de vivir que no dan de vivir," where the ragpicker, like the *castañera*, also takes her brandy. Bretón observes a custom, describes it, gives a social reason for change, and then returns to his festive air: "but if wine is pleasing with them, with chestnuts it is indispensable under pain of strangulation.... That dry floury substance, of most difficult and laborious swallowing, urgently demands wine, whence without doubt comes the popular saying: *dijo la castaña al vino, bien venido seas, amigo* ["said the chestnut to the wine, welcome, friend"]." (*Obras 1883*, V, 501).

Sarcastic and witty, Bretón's *castañera* is the repository of all the information and gossip on her block. She amuses herself with satire, but "she knows how to let out her barbs slyly and opportunely, and even the words she hawks her wares with are wont to be so many innuendoes of Father Cobos [broad hints]."[7] The last sentence of the article contains the *castañera's* wicked pun about the calorific content of her chestnuts and the scrivener's daughters: *Here they are, red hot now!*

II   The Scattered Works (Obra Dispersa)

Bretón wrote scores of articles for newspapers and magazines such as *El Correo Literario y Mercantil, La Aurora de España, Boletín del Comercio, La Abeja, La Ley, El Liceo Artístico y Literario, El Museo de las Familias, El Semanario Pintoresco, El Correo de Ultramar, La Moda, Revista de Ciencias, Literatura y Artes,* and *La América.*[8] Until recently these articles had not been collected or edited, but in 1965 J.M. Díez Taboada and M. M. Rozas published the first volume of a projected three volume work, namely, *Obra Dispersa, vol. I, El Correo Literario y Mercantil.* Volume II was to have contained "the articles scattered throughout other publications," and Volume III "the poetic work not already collected." It seems unlikely, however, that volumes II and III will be published.[9]

The articles of the *Correo Literario y Mercantil,* which first appeared between April 4, 1831, and October 9, 1833, are important documents for the history of the Spanish theater. They discuss forthcoming plays, the contracts of theatrical companies, news from the provinces and abroad — especially the dramas of Paris and operas of Italy — plays staged in private houses, the three unities, Romanticism, the use of rhyme, monologues, asides, the art of declamation, anachronisms, actors' costumes, short biographies and necrologies of famous singers and actors, economic problems, the "philharmonic fury," plays of magic, gymnastic exhibitions, pantomime, translations, *refundiciones,* Ventura de la Vega, Molière and Scribe, and much more. In short, they capture much of the theatrical activity of Spain during a period of two and a half years.

As for Bretón himself, these articles reveal the plight of a liberal accommodating himself to the reign of Ferdinand VII, who protected the *Correo Literario y Mercantil;* Bretón had to write laudatory pieces to Ferdinand and his bride, Doña María Cristina. Besides this praise, one constantly encounters the two pillars of his early theater — Moratín and the doctrine of verisimilitude. Anything is acceptable in the theater providing it is verisimilar, which explains his rejection of "literary Romanticism" ("el cólera morbo literario" he calls it). It is simply too far-fetched and lacking in verisimilitude.[10]

III *"The Art of Declamation"*

In 1832 Bretón published a brief article on "The Art of Declamation," in which he argued that it is difficult to reduce" this art to fixed principles. Then he wrote: "In any case, if it is possible to compose a treatise on theatrical declamation, we do not consider ourselves sufficiently enlightened to write it, nor would the limits of a newspaper[11] be able to hold it" (*Obra dispersa,* pp. 217-18). Twenty years later he had a change of heart, for he composed the long "Progress and Present State of the Art of Declamation in the Theaters of Spain." Written in 1852, this study was published in the Baudry edition of selected works of 1853.[12]

Bretón's treatise likens declamation to the other arts, for "imitation is the essence" of all of them. Then it gives a brief history of the theater in Spain down to Leandro Fernández de Moratín, "the regenerator of our theater." The bulk of the treatise examines Spanish nineteenth century theater from every aspect, but four main ideas are outstanding: First, "the progress of declamation in our country has been far too slow." (*Obras 1853,* I, xliv). Second, actors are born, not made, although the study of history and literature, a few rules concerning pronunciation and "other accessories of the profession," and the habit of "carefully analyzing roles so as to know the spirit of each verse, each sentence" will undoubtedly help the young actor. (*Obras 1853,* I, lx). The third and most important idea is drawn from the activity of one man, Isidoro Máiquez, who studied under Talma in France and single-handedly reformed the actor's art in Spain. The presence of Máiquez was so profound that he even changed the material conditions of the theater: actors' remuneration, the numbering of seats and the abolition of the *mosquetería,* the staging of plays at night, the abolition of "selling water and other trifles in the pit," the substitution of coaches for litters, in which the actresses had been carried "sometimes not without scandal." The pages concerning Máiquez are the most eminent of Bretón's prose works; no student of the nineteenth century theater should fail to read them. Bretón's final topic is his preference for versification in the theater. Of all enemies of good theater he most detests the *morcilleros,* those actors who freely change an author's verses while they are on stage.[13]

IV *The* Résumés of Acts and Deeds[14]

These documents, issued annually by Bretón as executive secretary of the Academy from 1860 to 1869, have informational rather than aesthetic value. In 1864–1865, for example, one learns that there will be more weekly meetings because of a literary contest and the preparation of a select library of classical authors; that in this library Hartzenbusch will prepare the *Quijote,* Bretón the *Fábulas* of Iriarte and Samaniego, Molíns the works of the mystics, Vega the theater of Moratín, Valera the Spanish writings of Portuguese authors and the *Amadís;* that Vega will receive an honorarium in spite of his absence; that 15,000 *reales* will go to the family of Nicomedes Pastor Díaz to substidize an edition of one of his books; that three companions have died, Mora, Alcalá Galiano, and Rivas, for whom necrologies will be read; that Adelardo López de Ayala has been named to the Academy; and that several books have been received. These documents throw light on the last decade of Bretón's life.[15]

V *The Poems*

Bretón wrote hundreds of poems throughout his life for several kinds of publication: pamphlets, loose sheets, political periodicals, and literary reviews. Many of his poems remained unpublished, and some were passed anonymously from hand to hand. When he finally collected his poems and published them as Volume V of the *Obras* of 1851, he suppressed many for artistic or other reasons.[16]

Bretón divided his poems into three groups, the satirical, the amatory, and the "compositions of elevated tone":

The satirical genre, which ... tends to be doctrinal, and here perhaps is precisely that, dominates in the present compilation, formulated now in tercets, now in *letrillas,* now in *romances.* It is the genre for which the editor has always felt the strongest inclination, and for which he considers himself the least inept.... Amatory and gallant verses also abound in this collection. The author has never professed to be a hermit, and he dares hope that no one will accuse him of coldness or affectation in his erotic outbursts, since his heart rather than his fantasy has the greater part in them. Finally, the compositions of more grave and elevated tone, if limited in value, for the author does not boast of being Pindaric, are few in number....[17]

By his own statement, Bretón is primarily a satirical rather than a lyrical poet. Thus his poems resemble his theater, for which they provide a good key; for example, Bretón's poems have many references to *talle,* the "philharmonic fury," translations, *refundiciones,* Carnival, the *ambigú,* coquettes, Moratín, etc.[18]

VI *The Satires*

Bretón calls ten of his tercets "Satires"; they ridicule the "philharmonic fury," superficial authors, artless actors, hypocrites, the new mania for travel, and assorted customs of the nineteenth century. Most of his numerous *letrillas* and *romances* are also satires, as well as the thousand verse *The Life of Man* and the sixty-five hundred verse *Shamelessness, A Jocular-Serious Poem (La desvergüenza, poema jocoserio),* written in *octavas reales.* A brief commentary on this last and longest poem will suffice to describe all his satires.

First, Bretón's verses have been called a philological monument containing the vocabulary and usages of Madrid chitchat.[19] They include the jargon of politicians and bankers; the *lengua franca* of fops and dandies; Gallicisms in abundance; Latin expressions still in vogue; the names of tools, fabrics, clothing, and common items of the period; household rhetoric — the unwritten literature of the day, so to speak. Briefly, they reveal the state of the vernacular.

Second, *Shamelessness* has many heterogeneous ideas rather than a single central one and consequently lacks unity. The twelve cantos wander freely, from an invocation to shamelessness, to a just reparation for women, *pandillaje* or mutual admiration, diplomacy, politics, commerce, literature, valor, honor, virtue, and miscellany. Unlike Bretón's plays, however, the poem does not have dramatic direction. Its main purpose strikes one as being formal rather than corrective or didactic; the author is enjoying his feats of versification, which are at times difficult.[20]

The third commentary resembles the second and may account for it. Bretón lacks the conviction and doggedness of a great satirist. He had written in one of his *romances:*

> And she [Thalia, the muse] gave me for the punishment
> of rogues and fools,
> the ferule of Menander
> without Aristophanes's ire. (*Obras 1883,* V, 250)

Bretón may write verses about bad poets and actors, awkward husbands, crooked politicians, social climbers, deceitful women, fops, mothers-in-law, and other annoyances, but one need only read Juvenal or Quevedo to see how he differs from them. His verses have no sharp teeth; he writes to delight, not to correct, and, as one critic put it, "Bretón does not excite to rebellion ... he doesn't know Juvenal even on the surface."[21]

VII The Amatory and Gallant Verses

In his love poetry, Bretón appears as a late disciple of the eighteenth century Salamantine school. His model is Anacreonte, the poet who sang of murmuring brooks, the rose of love, and the consolation of wine and friendship. He bestows pastoral names upon his friends — *Anfriso* (Alberto Lista), *Delio* (Ventura de la Vega), *Belardo* (Mesonero Romanos), and *Dalmiro* (Juan de la Pezuela) — as he speaks of his love for Laura, Rosaura, and Silvia:[22]

> The Rose
> Care, my Silvia, take care!
> Ay! not for a rose
> should thou risk
> thy tender hand to pain.
> . . . .
> Venus lived a hundred centuries
> boasting of her deed
> until thou wert born,
> oh shepherdess most fair.   (*Obras 1883*, V, 311)

As supreme goddess, Venus had made the roses by placing her foot on "the carpet green," but now love has brought two roses to Silvia's countenance and so Venus is jealous; she has surrounded the beautiful rose with cruel thorns among the lovely leaves. The poet tells the shepherdess not to pluck the rose for him lest she come to harm, but she replies: "What matters it that the thorn pierce me / if the rose is *for thee* alone?" (*Obras 1883*, V, 311).

In time Bretón abandoned this Neoclassical poetry for the more open *letrillas*, which read rather like popular songs:

Zagales, no es Flora	Lads, 'tis not Flor
La reina de Abril.	who's queen of the May.
No ahora	No more
la adora	do they adore
Su ledo pensil.	her the flowers in array.
. . . .	. . . .

Y ufana te admira	And proudly thou art admired
Cual reina de Abril	as queen of the May
Mi lira	by my lyre
que inspira	inspired
Tu talle gentil.	by thy graceful form.

(*Obras 1883,* V, 135)

VIII Translations, Adaptations, Miscellany

Before concluding this book, we should consider several other plays of our prolific author: (1) his numerous translations and *refundiciones,* (2) his tragedies, (3) his *zarzuelas* (operatic or lyrical dramas), (4) his "great comedy of magic," and (5) his last play, *The Bodily Senses* (*Los sentidos corporales,* 1867).

Bretón translated some seventy-seven plays, two from the Italian, the rest from the French. He translated authors such as Racine (two plays), Scribe (thirteen plays), le Franc de Pompignan, Alfieri, Marivaux (two plays), Beaumarchais, Hugo, and Molière, besides a score of less famous French authors. One might note his many translations of Augustin Eugène Scribe (1791-1861), to whom he has been compared: S. T. Wallis, for example, writing in 1853, calls him "The Scribe of Spain."[23] Quantitatively, the comparison is justifiable, since Bretón produced plays in Scribian numbers, but qualitatively, the Bretonian *comedia* differs from the well-made play of Scribe and others (e.g., the *Verre d'Eau* with its effects and causes). Perhaps this is what Le Gentil had in mind when he wrote:

The irresistible drollery of Bretón's plays escapes analysis. If one tries, nevertheless, to separate their elements, in the first place they appear to hold to a design, to the capacity of the author not to complicate the plots — which Scribe and the dramatic carpenters would consider to be the high point of all art — but rather to simplify the plots so as to regulate the proportions harmoniously and symmetrically.[24]

Scribe wrote about a country that his critics dubbed *Scribia,*[25] where structures are put together as in carpentry, but Bretón wrote about a country called Spain.

The Spanish impresarios of Bretón's day were constantly looking for new material to offer the Madrid audiences, who were demanding more and more entertainment. In addition to original plays, translations from the French, and Italian opera, another source of material was the *comedia* of Spain's Golden Age (the theater of the sixteenth and seventeenth centuries), the modern adaptations of which were called *refundiciones*. Bretón wrote ten such adaptations, two of plays by Lope de Vega, four by Calderón, and one each by Tirso de Molina, Coello, Moreto, and Ruiz de Alarcón. In adapting them to the nineteenth century stage, he strove above all for simplicity and clarity; for example, he shortens Lope's *¡Si no vieran las mujeres!* by about one-third, completely removing its Baroque amazement and conceits. He extracts the essential action of this labyrinthine comedy and then tells the love story of Federico and Isabela and the former's conflict with Emperor Otón, who lusts after Federico's betrothed. Bretón's study of Golden Age plays was responsible for his insistence on versification in the theater; consequently, the *refundiciones* of 1826–1831 (only two were written after this time) were an important part of his dramatic education.[26]

Bretón translated nine tragedies and wrote two of his own, *Romeo and Juliet* (1830) and *Mérope* (1835). I have not seen the former, which exists only in manuscript form, and, according to Bretón's nephew, "is preserved in the hands of the author's heirs"[27] (see *Obras 1883*, I, xxii). *Mérope, A Tragedy In Three Acts,* was included in volume I of the collected *Obras* of 1850. Contrary to Bretón's announcement and the readers' expectations, it is not a tragedy, but a drama ending well with the coronation of Egisto and homage paid to Mérope.

In trying his hand at tragedy, Bretón was following a bias of the day, namely, that tragedy is more noble, edifying, and moral than other theatrical genres.[28] Thus, Vega wrote his *Muerte de César;* Tamayo, *Virginia;* Martínez de la Rosa, *Edipo;* Quintana, *Pelayo;* Pacheco, *Alfredo;* and so forth. None of these tragedies is held in the same esteem today as Moratín's comedy, *El sí de las niñas,* or Bretón's *Die and You Will See! (Muérete ¡y verás!).*

Spain has had a long history of musical dramas (*zarzuelas*), dating back to Calderón in the seventeenth century and to antecedent sixteenth century authors such as Juan del Encina and Lucas Fernández. These dramas acquired a popular character in the eighteenth century with the *zarzuelas* of Ramón de la Cruz, but by the time of Cruz's death in 1794 they had declined to the point of near extinction.[29] It is significant that Mariano José de Larra in *El rapto* (1832) and Bretón in *El novio y el concierto* (1839) served as playwrights-librettists in the revival of the art,[30] which differs from opera. An opera is sung in its entirety, whereas a *zarzuela* is a play or *sainete* with some parts spoken and others that may be sung; its music is ordinarily lighter and more popular than an opera's.[31]

Bretón himself wrote the play and book for four *zarzuelas,* namely, *The Fiancé and Music* (*El novio y el concierto,* 1839), *The Loners* (*Los solitarios,* 1843), *The Parboiled Fiancé,* (*El novio pasado por agua,* 1852), and *Don Juan's Business* (*Cosas de Don Juan,* 1854). Nevertheless, he showed disdain for this genre by excluding the last two *zarzuelas,* in three acts, from his collected *Obras* of 1883, "since I was commissioned to do both works and since I don't like the genre they belong to; and also because the success of both works is something I cannot pride myself on, even though they weren't hissed" (*Obras 1883,* I, lxiv).[32] Perhaps when Bretón wrote these words, as he was preparing the *Plan* for a posthumous edition of his works, he had in mind the harsh criticism journalists like Alarcón were heaping on the *zarzuelas*,[33] and he was being apologetic. But it is our privilege to disagree with him. *The Parboiled Fiancé* is superior to many allegedly serious plays of Bretón, such as *Independence* (*La Independencia,* 1844), *The Worthy Woman* (*El valor de la mujer,* 1852), and *Birds of a Feather* (*La cabra tira al monte,* 1853); and it is far more representative than they of Bretonian comedy.

The theme of *The Fiancé and Music* is presented simply and clearly. A young beau, Luis, becomes disenchanted with his bride-to-be, Remigia, who always sings arias only in Italian, and he falls in love with her Cinderella cousin, Laura, whom he hears singing spontaneously in Spanish. Remigia is spoiled and fastidious, whereas Laura is modest and free. Luis's uncle Lupercio engages in a contest with Remigia, the latter singing serious opera in Italian, the former singing *ópera bufa* and Andalusian *jácaras* in Spanish. At times they sing a half-jocular, half-serious duet in the two languages, an unusual accomplishment in keeping with the principal goal of the play: music versus music. This *zarzuela* develops theatrically the satirical poem Bretón had written back in 1828, "Against the Philharmonic Furor, Or Rather, Against Those Who Scorn Spanish Theater." It is ironic that Bretón, wanting to defend Spanish music and theater in the face of the overwhelming glory of Italian opera in Spain, teamed up with the Italian composer Basilio Basili. The son of another famous composer, Francisco Basili, Basilio had come to Spain as a young man; he wrote both the Italian and Spanish scores of Bretón's play.[34]

The most popular Spanish play of the nineteenth century before the appearance of José Zorrilla's *Don Juan Tenorio* was *The Goat's Foot* (*La pata de cabra*) by Juan de Grimaldi. Zorrilla, whose father was superintendent of police when the play was staged, had this to say: "It was absolutely prohibited for all Spaniards from the provinces to come to Madrid without a justified reason, and the superintendent put a visa, written in favor of the bearers, on 72,000 passports for this powerful and unimpeachable reason: "Entrance granted to Madrid to see *The Goat's Foot*."[35] Bretón reviewed *The Goat's Foot* in August of 1831 and again in November of 1832 for the *Correo literario y mercantil*.[36]

Grimaldi's spectacle was a *comedia de magia,* a magic play, relying heavily on stage tricks, "the principal laurel"[37] of such an entertainment. *The Goat's Foot* abounded in metamorphoses, sorcery, magnificent decorations, dances, songs, people flying, jokes, and reptiles vomiting flames. It came close to being pure circus. Its dramatic pretensions, such as they were, consisted of nothing more than the accumulation of events leading up to the marriage of a boy and girl.

As one might suppose, many authors imitated *The Goat's Foot* (whose success at the box office was incredible, a million *reales* in four years) — for example, Hartzenbusch in 1839 and 1841, Bretón in 1831[38] and 1841, and Tamayo y Baus in 1853. Bretón called the *comedia de magia* "a bastard genre," adding that a poet must sacrifice a great deal and subordinate "the interests of Thalia to mechanical laws, poetic inspiration to optical tricks, sentiment to depth perception, the heart to the senses; the plot to stage machinery ["la trama a la tramoya"], truth to the absurd; and the grace of dialogue to pretense" (*Obras 1850,* III, 303, note). He wrote *The Marvelous Plume (La pluma prodigiosa)* in 1841, to please the Madrid public, with whom he was losing popularity. Bretón's magic play is filled with Moslems and sultans; beards, moustaches, and turbans that come flying off faces; a beheaded duenna; armies of *moriscos;* a seraglio; a palace beneath the sea; dungeons; and so forth, but in the end, as one might expect in a Bretonian comedy, the young man finds he wants the young girl "in holy wedlock." And he need not travel around the world to learn this true philosophy.[39]

Bretón terminated his career with two plays staged when he was past seventy: *The Poor Man's Advocate (El abogado de pobres),* in 1866, and *The Bodily Senses (Los sentidos corporales),* in 1867. He had written his first play, *The Young Old Codger,* in 1817, in a

Spain that was vastly different. But in spite of the fifty year span, Bretonian *comedia* from start to finish has basically the same twofold nature: (1) a festive air, and (2) young love's overcoming all impediments.

The battle between the bodily senses (*los sentidos corporales*) and the spirit is the theme of Bretón's last play, and indeed, of his theater as a corpus. This does not imply that the body is evil and must be subdued by a self-death, a sort of *endura,* but rather the opposite. Act I of Bretón's last play glorifies the five senses, which the characters debate in a poetic contest: Flora praises spring with its aromas; Filomeno, music and song; Adolfo, the joys of taste; Angela, the sight of the stars and the snows of Moncayo; and Desiderio, the nobility of touch.[40] In Bretón the senses are good, and a beautiful woman is the crown of creation, but left to themselves they are incomplete. They must be exalted by the breath of spirit, which is best realized in *santo himeneo,* holy wedlock (a phrase often repeated by Bretón).

Bretón ends this, his last play, with these fitting words of the erstwhile misanthrope, Don Bruno, who praises Angela:

> I see happily united in her
> — they are so many and so great! —
> sweet charms and pure
> for the soul and for the senses.[41]   (Act III, scene vii)

IX *Conclusion and Summation, and a Proper Epitaph*

The dramatist Manuel Bretón de los Herreros (1796–1873) has been likened by French critics to their own novelist, Honoré de Balzac (1799–1850). They have said that Bretón's hundred-odd plays are "a complete tableau, often charming, of society in the times of Doña Cristina and Doña Isabel"; they have also observed that he will always be the foremost comic playwright of Spain in the nineteenth century, "the Balzac of the Spanish bourgeoisie from 1830 to 1860."[42] Lest it seem unusual for the principal playwright of one country to be compared to the novelist of another, we should remember that Fernán Caballero did not publish her novel, *The Seagull (La gaviota)* until 1849 and that the novel did not come into its own in Spain until 1868, when Galdós began his illustrious career. Thus, in the 1830s and 1840s Bretón was writing the Spanish human comedy for the stage, in verse, whereas Balzac was writing

Of Opuscules and Poetry: Tying Up Loose Ends 133

the French human comedy as a novel, in prose. With his insistence on the use of verse, which he spelled out in his Academy speech of 1837, Bretón was instinctively adapting an old form, the Golden Age *comedia,* to a new subject — nineteenth century civilization, with its changing social order and penchant for realism. He was the last bulwark of an ancient tradition, since Manuel Tamayo y Baus (1829-1898) abandoned the verse of his earlier plays for prose, and Enrique Gaspar (1842-1902), a fine versifier, came to deprecate verses in the theater.[43] Finally, Spain's most eminent modern novelist, Benito Pérez Galdós (1843-1920), by adapting his novels for the stage, in prose, also became her most eminent playwright for two decades.

Although an ardent student and admirer of seventeenth century authors, Bretón was rarely as musical as they. One must study him in his dialogues rather than his lyrics, whereas a playwright like Lope de Vega is both a lyric and dramatic poet. Bretón also admired the Neoclassical comedies of Moratín (1760-1828), whose simplicity and clarity he found most refreshing during the early years of the nineteenth century, when outlandish dramas prevailed in the theater. Always devoted to Moratín, he nevertheless broke somewhat with his Neoclassical restraint in 1831, with *Marcela*. Bretonian comedy may be considered an amalgam of seventeenth century theater, shorn of its lyric poetry and conceits, and of the limpid plays of Moratín, set in a nineteenth century middle class environment.

His stage manner, unlike the profound bitterness of his own later personal life, was almost always cheerful. He strikes his reader as being festive, with a twinkle in his eye.[44] His plays abound in young lovers successfully defying their elders, the *senex* figures, who are more interested in wealth and obedience than happy marriages. A young man has a certain physical and spiritual form (*talle*), as does a young lady, and when both forms are in harmony, heaven and nature conspire for their union, which all the meddlesome parents and relatives in the world cannot prevent. Bretón sets this story of young love against the background of his society, for example, the Carlist civil war, the newspaper world, the political arena, a boarding house, home and hearth, life in the provinces, life in the city, a masked ball, a fishing village, an army camp, a country home, a street corner, a drawing room, and similar scenes.

In addition to his Bretonian comedy, Bretón wrote every type of play in vogue between the 1820s and 1860s: tragedies, *zarzuelas,* historical dramas, the magic play, a Romantic drama, anti-Romantic satires, one act plays, translations, adaptations, and even incipient *alta comedia*. Most of these works serve to mark off the others; the person reading Bretón's five score works will soon learn to distinguish and think: "this is Bretonian comedy" *Die and You Will See! (Muérete ¡y verás!), Marcela, The Country bumpkin (El pelo de la dehesa), The Newspaper (La redacción de un periódico), The Editor Responsible (El editor responsable), Foibles of State (Flaquezas ministeriales);* whereas "the others are plays written by Bretón": *Dido, Elena, Vellido Dolfos, Independence* (La Independencia), *In Arrears (Cuentas atrasadas), Birds of a Feather (La cabra tira al monte).* A play such as *The Girl at the Counter (La niña del mostrador)* is a hybrid — half Bretonian and half Scribian or Tamayesque.

Bretón has been vastly underrated as an author, as a sort of merry andrew, or Scribian contriver, or simply another mediocre playwright of the nineteenth century, a time when "Spanish plays were merely the libretti for Italian opera."[45] But he deserves a more conscientious criticism. He rarely employed the sentimentalism and cloying tone of later nineteenth century authors, nor was he accustomed to writing melodramas. He only criticized vices against nature, which may be reduced to hypocrisy, and so he most resembles the author of *Tartuffe,* Molière.[46]

What is a fitting epitaph for Bretón, a phrase to sum up his life and literature? Several sayings come to mind, from his critics, from his comedies, and from the writings of other authors. Here are some examples:

From Bretón's critics:

He rediscovered the vein of national mirth.
—Charles de Mazade[47]

The poet writes the way everyone speaks. He writes for
  the middle class.
—Georges LeGentil[48]

From Bretón's own works:

> This may be in poor fashion
> and common, and whatever else...;
> but it's the fruit of my country,
> and I am very Spanish.
> — *Obras 1883,* V, 292.

Of Opuscules and Poetry: Tying Up Loose Ends

> I portray for you the Spain of today
> as I see it, I swear.
> — *Obras 1883,* V, 349.

> Nations want variety in their theater.
> — *Obra dispersa,* p. 67.

> The friendship of man and woman always becomes
> ambiguous.
> — *Obras 1883,* IV, 397.

And here are some sayings, taken from other authors, which could be used as epitaphs for Bretón:

> What forbids a man
> to tell the truth by laughter?
> Horace[49]

> Almost always laughing
> very rarely crying
> to correct manners
> delighting.
> — Modesto Lafuente[50]

But the most apt phrase I have seen for summing up the meaning of Bretón's existence comes from Spain's famous poet and critic, Dámaso Alonso (1898-   ):[51]

> God is also seen in the pretty eyes of a girl.

Notes and References

Chapter One

1. See the Marqués de Molíns, *Bretón de los Herreros* (Madrid, 1883), p. xiii, and Hartzenbusch's prologue to Bretón's *Obras escogidas* (Paris, 1853), I, xiv (hereafter cited as *Obras 1853*). See also Bretón's *Obra dispersa* (Logroño, 1965), pp. 202, 447. Bretón's *vis cómica* is defined in Molíns, p. 163.

2. Bretón, *Obras* (Madrid, 1883-1884), V, 105, 321 (hereafter cited as *Obras 1883*). See also Georges Le Gentil, *Le Poète Manuel Bretón de los Herreros* (Paris, 1909), p. 17; Molíns, pp. 297-98; and Juan Valera, *Obras completas* (Madrid, 1961), II, 1276. In 1841, in a poem to the actor Julián Romea, Bretón jested about his eyes: "even in this I am singular."

3. The old man and girl theme comes proximately from the plays of Moratín and ultimately from the tradition of all comedy. See the argument concerning *senex* figures in J.L. Calderwood and H.E. Toliver, *Perspectives in Drama* (New York, 1968), pp. 163-76.

4. The word *cursi* did not come into use until approximately 1865, but Bretón's plays show that the reality preceded the verbal expression by at least thirty years.

5. There are, for example, very few references to Bretón in the annual bibliography of the PMLA.

6. One must beware of a post hoc argument. See the names of José Martínez Ruiz (Azorín) and Carmen de Burgos, in the bibliography.

7. A revision has started with the articles in the 1947 edition of the journal *Berceo* and the 1968 dissertation of Silva Novo Chaskin (see the *Selected Bibliography*). Much remains to be done, however.

8. *Obras 1883*, V, 530; see also the poem "Mi Lugar" on p. 249. Quel is described in the article of J. García Prado, "Bretón y su patria chica," *Berceo*, II (1947), 57-62.

9. The *Quel-¿Qué?* thought is Bretón's own: if you don't stress the letter *l*, he says, people think you answer *What?* when they ask where you are from.

10. Molíns says December 19, but Le Gentil says the 18th and quotes a birth certificate from the parish registry.

11. Le Gentil, p. 4. See also p. 8 of the 1905 edition of Bretón's *¿Quién es ella?*, edited by Samuel Garner.

12. Bretón did not retain the Latin learned at this time and had to study it later as an adult. He was an indefatigable worker.

Notes and References

13. In the *Obras 1883*, I, v, Cándido Bretón y Orozco, Bretón's nephew, gives a good account of his uncle's army career. Le Gentil, p. 12, explains why Bretón never rose beyond the rank of corporal.
14. The *alojamiento* appears in *La Independencia* (1844) and *La cabra tira al monte* (1853).
15. Le Gentil, pp. 9–14.
16. J.A. Corey, "The Comedies of Manuel Bretón de los Herreros" (Ann Arbor, 1973), p. 37. Bretón must have joked about his affliction; e.g., the following verses made the rounds of the Parnasillo: "—Una víbora picó / a Manuel Bretón, el tuerto. / — ¿Murió Bretón? — No, por cierto / La víbora reventó." See Antonio Espina, *Romea* (Madrid, 1935), p. 59; and Le Gentil, p. 14; also Narciso Alonso Cortés, *Bretón de los Herreros, Teatro* (Madrid, 1943), pp. xx–xxii. Alonso Cortés ascribes these jocular verses to Juan Martínez Villergas.
17. *Obras 1883*, V, 504; the article is called "La Castañera." The "famous person of the court of Charles IV" is Manuel Godoy, who died in 1851, eight years after the article was written.
18. Raymond Carr has offered a revision of the critical attitude toward Ferdinand's reign; see his, *Spain 1808–1939* (Oxford, 1966), pp. 146–49. For more ideas concerning the middle class of this era, See Juan Martínez Villergas, *Juicio crítico* (Paris, 1954), p. 39; Henry David Inglis, *Spain* (London, 1837), I, 113, 118, 122; Corey, pp. 45, 50–51; and Leandro Fernández de Moratín, *Orígenes del teatro español* (Paris: Garnier, n.d.), p. 467, the sentence beginning: "Busqué en la clase media de la sociedad los argumentos---"
19. See the opinion of Hartzenbusch in Bretón *Obras 1853*, II, xii.
20. Bretón wrote *A la vejez viruelas* in 1817, while on military leave. It was not staged until 1824.
21. By "eight major contributions" I mean seven full-length comedies and a tragedy. A list of Bretón's plays compiled by his nephew appears in *Obras 1883*, I, xx–xxix.
22. A month was a very long run at this time since most plays were performed only for a few days. Le Gentil, p. 20, citing Molíns, says that Bretón received "300 reales or one ounce of gold" for *A Madrid me vuelvo*.
23. *Obras 1883*, I, 61, as quoted in Corey, p. 66. Le Gentil, p. 26, lists all the translations by Bretón. See also *Obras 1853*, II, xxi.
24. See Bretón, *Obras* (Madrid, 1850–1851), I, 1 (hereafter cited as *Obras 1850*).
25. See *Obra dispersa*, p. 11.
26. *Obras 1883*, V, 17. See also Gabriel Lovett's article, "Francophobia in Nineteenth Century Spanish Letters," *Kentucky Romance Quarterly*, XIX (1972), 285–99.
27. *Obra dispersa*, pp. 171–73.
28. Concerning his early versification, see the brief biography by

Antonio Gil y Zárate, in Nicomedes Pastor Díaz, *Galería de españoles célebres contemporáneos* (Madrid, 1841), pp. 1-53.

29. Concerning the *alta comedia,* see Gerard Flynn, *Manuel Tamayo y Baus* (New York, 1973), p. 155.

30. The *Obras 1850* call *Mérope* a tragedy, and in the *Obras 1883* Cándido Bretón lists it as such. It is not really a tragedy because of its "happy" ending.

31. However, his own *comedia* was Bretón's first love: "Toute sa vie le poète a lutté contre l'écrasante concurrence du melodrame, du drame historique, de l'opérette andalouse. Jamais il n'a tenu son public. Il en a souffert jusqu'à la mort." Le Gentil, pp. 35, 38.

32. See José Montero Alonso, *Ventura de la Vega* (Madrid, 1951), p. 127. According to Molíns, pp. 185-86 and 385-86, Bretón keenly felt the attacks of hostile critics. And see Alonso Cortés's edition of Bretón's *Teatro,* p. xxi.

33. In her doctoral dissertation, Silvia Novo Chaskin argues that Larra and Bretón were in personality greatly unlike each other; see p. 101, 168, 175-76. Molíns (p. 103) says their friendship was "never very solid."

34. Concerning Bretón's wife, see Chaskin, pp. 18-19, and 194-97. Molíns, his close friend, says that "one of the sorrows of that good man was not to have children" (pp. 308-309).

35. The speed of his acceptance may be an Academy record. A man like Tamayo y Baus took a year to prepare his speech, Galdós some eight years!

36. Other works concerning Carlism are *Los carlistas en Portugal* (1834), *El plan de un drama* (1835), *Otro diablo predicador* (1835), and *Pascual y Carranza* (1843). See Chaskin, p. 20; Molíns, p. 295; Le Gentil, pp. 41, 195, 287; and Corey, p. 38.

37. Under the spoils system of the Spanish civil service there were many *cesantes,* persons put out of office and hence unemployed. Benito Pérez Galdós wrote a famous novel, *Miau,* on this subject.

38. The letter is dated May 16, 1843; see Molíns, pp. 360-61. Concerning Bretón's bitterness see ibid., pp. 158, 258, 260, 308-309, 512; Valera, II, 1275; Chaskin, p. 220, Enrique Piñeyro, *El romanticismo en España* (Paris, 1934), pp. 212-14, 218-20; and Le Gentil, p. 48: "cette amertume qui dès lors empoisonne sa vie, le rendant songeur et maussade."

39. Many of Bretón's friends died during this period: the Duke of Frías in 1851, the actor Romea in 1863, and Ventura de la Vega and the Duke of Rivas in 1865. Vega was "le plus aimé des confrères" (Le Gentil, p. 51).

40. Were the reader not advised of Bretón's malaise, he might expect him to be the most contented of men in later life. By all accounts, he was financially successful.

41. Eusebio Blasco, "Las costumbres en el teatro, "*La España del Siglo XIX, Curso de 1886-1887,* III, 154, has a description of Bretón in his old age. See also Manuel Mesonero Romanos, *Las sepulturas de los hombres*

ilustres (Madrid, 1898), pp. 33-35, which includes a picture of Bretón's gravestone.

Chapter Two

1. Northrop Frye, *Anatomy of Criticism* (Princeton, 1973), pp. 33-35.
2. See Calderwood and Toliver, pp. 165-67. For an explicit reference to the *senex,* see Bretón's one act *El hombre pacífico* (scene xv): "¿En qué fundas tu derecho, / senectud?"
3. Doña Francisca resembles somewhat the *lindo don Diego* (the pretty don Diego; the dandy) of Agustín Moreto; see *El lindo don Diego,* Act II, scene x.
4. Doña Francisca's attitude toward Spain recalls Joaquín Bartrina's (1850-1880) famous verses: "Hearing a man speak, it is easy / to ascertain where he saw the light of day; / if he praises England he must be English; / if he condemns Prussia he must be French; / and if he speaks ill of Spain then he is Spanish." See Pío Baroja, *El árbol de la ciencia,* ed. by Gerard Flynn (New York: Appleton-Century, 1970), p. 269.
5. The word *cursi* was not yet in vogue, but she is like a character from Jacinto Benavente's *Lo cursi* (1901). See Fernando Díaz-Plaja, *La vida española en el siglo XIX* (Madrid, 1952), p. 115.
6. See Díaz-Plaja, p. 163.
7. See Charles B. Qualia, "The *Raisonneur* in the Social Drama of Spain," *Hispania,* XIX (1936), 407-14.
8. See Lafragua's analysis of *The Young Old Codger* in his 1842 edition of Bretón, *Teatro* (México, 1842), I, 101-103 (hereafter cited as *Teatro 1842*). The phrase "a la vejez viruelas," which appears in Bretón's *Cuidado con las amigas* (Act I, scene ix) and in Moratín's *El viejo y la niña* (Act II, scene i), literally means "chicken pox in old age."
9. Lafragua has an analysis of *The Two Nephews* in *Teatro 1842,* I, 295-96.
10. See J. Hunter Peak, *Social Drama in Nineteenth-Century Spain* (Chapel Hill, 1964), pp. 41-43. See also Chaskin, pp. 51-57; Piñeyro, p. 204; Molíns, p. 277; and Lafragua's analysis in the *Teatro 1842,* II.
11. I construe *oscureciendo* as 5 P.M. or so. Thus Bretón's play begins at 7 A.M. and ends at 5 P.M., whereas Moratín's *El sí de las niñas* begins at 7 P.M. and ends at 5 A.M.; both take place in a similar ten hour period. Bretón was imitating Moratín in his time scheme.
12. See Lope de Vega's *Arte nuevo de hacer comedias:* "for this variety is most delightful. / A good example is given us by nature, / who through her great variety has beauty." (Verses 179-180; see *Arte nuevo de hacer comedias en este tiempo* (Madrid, 1971), p. 291.) Cf. Bretón's *Arte de la declamación* in *Obras 1853,* I, xl.
13. In 1539, Antonio de Guevara published his *Menosprecio de corte y alabanza de aldea (Scorn of City and Praise of Country Town).* Many

nineteenth century authors, especially the *costumbristas* (local color writers), might be called Guevarists.

14. *Albayalde* means "ceruse" or a cosmetic made of white lead.

15. *Ensanche:* the pun here escapes translation. *Ensanche* means *enlargement:* formerly a seamstress, the marquesa has enlarged her position in society. *Ensanche* also means the extra material behind the seam of a garment. We might call her the Marquesa of Highercut, or Marchioness of Granderfrills.

16. In Spanish, "dando gato por liebre" ("giving cat for hare") means "cheating by giving an inferior product of like kind."

17. See Díaz-Plaja, p. 17.

18. Bretón was familiar with the Horatian concept of *dulcis et utile,* which the Golden Age Spaniards (Tirso, Cervantes, etc.) rendered as *deleitar enseñando;* for him art was never mere entertainment. See Hartzenbusch's commentary on this question in his prologue to Bretón's *Obras 1853,* I, xi.

19. See E.K. Rand, *Founders of the Middle Ages* (Cambridge, 1941), ch. 4.

20. Leo Spitzer writes: "For what Cervantes did was *to posit the problem of the book,* and of its influence on life.... After Cervantes, many writers, Molière, Rousseau, Goethe, Chateaubriand, Nietzsche, and the Flaubert of *Madame Bovary* ... will exercise the right of the 'literary politician' to sift traditional literature and to pronounce a verdict on that part of literature which they believe has, in the process of time, become detrimental to the community." Spitzer, "On The Significance of Don Quixote," in Lowry Nelson, ed., *Cervantes, A Collection of Critical Essays* (Englewood Cliffs, 1969), pp. 85-86. In *The Phony Education,* Bretón is exercising the right of "literary politician," which was bequeathed to him by Cervantes, among others.

21. Oscar Wilde had three rules for writing plays: "The first rule is not to write like Henry Arthur Jones, the second and third rules are the same!" One could not direct such a barb at Bretón. See Doris Arthur Jones, *The Life and Letters of Henry Arthur Jones* (London, 1930), p. 187.

22. See Qualia.

23. Teresa is the girl with the pretty eyes (*Obras 1850,* I, 165: "los rayos de esos ojos"), but as an incorrigible coquette she does not win her man. Hence she is not included with the heroines of the four plays studied above.

24. "The bulk of the theatrical fare" consisted of awful melodramas such as those of Comella, reworked *comedias* of the Golden Age, and translations from the French. See Moratín's satirical play *La comedia nueva* in *Teatro completo* (Madrid, 1944); and see Charles Blaise Qualia's "Dramatic Criticism in the Comedies of Bretón de los Herreros," *Hispania,* XXIV (1941), 71-78, where *El ingenuo* and other plays are discussed.

Notes and References

25. See Jacques Marie Monvel, *L'Amant Bourru* (14 Août 1777), in *Chefs-D'Oeuvre des Auteurs Comiques* (Paris, 1879).
26. I have in my files a card marked "Nineteenth Century" with a score of pejorative references to that century taken from Bretón's plays. Some of the other plays noted there are *La falsa ilustración, La familia del boticario* (translation from the French), *Mocedades, A Madrid me vuelvo, La cabra tira al monte,* and *La niña del mostrador.* There are also references to Bretón's poetry: *Obras 1883,* V, 11, 83, 98, 355. See also Le Gentil, p. 261; Molíns, p. 372; and Chaskin, pp. 122, 189, 191, 192, 226.

Chapter Three

1. See *Obras 1853,* I, xxxvi; the full title of the essay is *Progresos y estado actual del arte de la declamación en los teatros de España.* Plautus faced the same obstacle of censorship and unities as Bretón: see Eric Segal, *Roman Laughter* (Cambridge, 1968), p. 9.
2. See *Los sentidos corporales* (Madrid, 1867), p. 93: "...El censor de teatros, Narciso S. Serra." Serra's appointment as censor seems in keeping with the canon's advice in the 1605 edition of Cervantes' *Quixote,* ch. 48. In any case, later censorship was more benign, or less malign, than *censura frailera.*
3. *Obras 1850,* I, 161.
4. See Molíns, pp. xiii, 163; also Hartzenbusch's prologue, *Obras 1853,* I, xiv.
5. See *Obras 1883,* I, lxii.
6. In *Achaques a los vicios,* the conflict arises between a vain wife, gluttonous mother-in-law, and gambling husband. In *Achaques* the conflict takes place after marriage.
7. I use "practical man" in the sense of "Bretón the playwright." See Harold Rosenberg, "The Profession of Poetry and M. Maritain," in *The Tradition of the New* (New York, 1965), pp. 96–120.
8. Concerning Don Zoilo's comic repetition, see Henri Bergson, *Laughter* (Garden City, 1956), pp. 67, 107, 120–22.
9. Although Bretón's early, Moratinian, plays passed censorship, Moratín's own plays were not granted staging for more than ten years. See A. Rumeau, "Le Théâtre à Madrid à la veille du Romantisme, 1831-1834," in *Hommage à Ernest Martinenche* (Paris, 1939), p. 341.
10. See Bergson, where *risible* is defined in the double sense of he who laughs and he who is laughed at.
11. By 1828 Bretón had already made adaptations of Lope, Calderón, and Moreto, and he recast a Ruiz de Alarcón play in 1829. He was well versed in the classical theater of Spain. By 1828 he had likewise translated the plays of Molière, Marivaux, and other French playwrights.
12. Apparently the merry andrew accusation is the fate of all comediographers, even of an author such as Molière. See F. Brunetière, *Brune-*

tière's Essays in French Literature (New York, 1898), pp. 67-72.

13. Molíns, ch. XIII.

14. See Segal. Much of what Segal says of Plautus can be predicated of Bretón.

15. George Meredith, *An Essay on Comedy* (Garden City, 1956), pp. 50-52.

16. Bergson, p. 117.

17. See "Cuatro consejos a un poeta dramático bisoño," in *Obras 1850,* V, 615; "The public does not limit its pleasures now to *bread and circuses,* which it was satisfied with in the ominous decade [1823-1833]."

18. Bergson, pp. 63-64.

19. Ibid.

20. There is no *comedia corregidora,* which is tantamount to saying there is no *comedia*. A perfect illustration of the censor appears in Molíns, pp. 46-47.

21. See also Juan Goytisolo's article, "Writing in an Occupied Language," *New York Times Book Review,* March 31, 1974, p. 47.

22. See Pedro Gómez Aparicio, *Historia del periodismo español* (Madrid, 1967), pp. 195-96.

23. See Severn Treackle Wallis, *Spain* (Boston, 1853), pp. 82-83. Wallis's Chapter IX concerns the press and newspapers, his Chapter XIX the theaters and dramatic literature.

24. See Calderwood and Tolliver, pp. 163-76.

25. Bretón himself wrote for the *Correo literario y mercantil:* see the articles in *Obra dispersa*. And see Fernando José de Larra, *La sociedad española a través del teatro del siglo XIX* (Madrid, 1947), p. 23.

26. See Gómez Aparicio, pp. 605-13.

27. The plays of Bretón frequently display an onomastic joy similar to that of Galdós' novels. Witness, for example this list of newspapers.

28. The name *Don Tadeo* calls to mind the real life Don Francisco Tadeo Calomarde, whose servile ways were like Don Fabricio's. Perhaps this likeness is not accidental and Bretón is calling on every resource at his command to reproduce the atmosphere of the period.

29. Manuel Tamayo y Baus, a Carlist, complains about the vile nature of newspapers in his moralizing plays of the 1850s and 1860s. And in 1853, Mr. Severn Treackle Wallis wrote about "certain encroachments on the privileges of the fourth estate" (p. 83). Wallis's argument suggests that there was less censorship before the fact of publication than punishment after it.

30. There is a fine article on the "editor responsable" in the *Enciclopedia Ilustrada* of Espasa-Calpe, vol. 19, p. 91, which quotes Cánovas del Castillo's "preámbulo al Real decreto de 31 de Diciembre de 1876," the source of my quotation.

31. See Rupert Allen, "The Romantic Element in *Muérete ¡y verás!*" *Hispanic Review,* XXXIV (1966), 218-27.

Notes and References 143

32. The play is set in Paris, a disguise perhaps to spare Bretón entanglement with the authorities. It is an extremely thin disguise, for the only thing French about the play is the name *Dupré* and the mention of a bribe in francs. In any case, such a comedy would not have been tolerated just nine years earlier, in the days of Ferdinand VII.

33. Concerning censorship, the reader might also study another play of Bretón, *Foibles of State* (*Flaquezas ministeriales,* 1838), which shows corruption and deviousness amongst highly placed officials.

34. Absolutism implies perfection, for the absolute by definition is perfect. An absolutist king may be taken as God's temporal vicar on earth.

35. The vicious: specifically, the hypocrites. See Brunetière's essay on Molière.

36. I myself had seen a resemblance to Balzac before reading Le Gentil's passage likening him to the great French novelist (p. 515), so there may be some truth to the thought. J. A. Corey disagrees (p. 18.) (The material of Chapter 3 has appeared in *Estudos Ibero-Americanos,* II, dez. 1976).

Chapter Four

1. See Molíns, pp. 187-88, 519; and see Eugenio Ochoa y Ronna, *Apuntes para una biblioteca de escritores contemporáneos,* Tomo I (Paris, 1840), p. 123.

2. Molíns, pp. 190-91.

3. Concerning the use of versification in drama: the playwright Enrique Gaspar (1842-1902) took an opposite position from that of Bretón. See Daniel Poyán Díaz, *Enrique Gaspar* (Madrid, 1957), II, 58-81. See also Ramón Pérez de Ayala, "Teatro en verso y teatro poético," in *Las Máscaras* (Madrid, 1924), II, 59-70: "It seems natural then that verse be employed in comic and humorous theater."

Chapter Five

1. The dandy, or *lechuguino, currutaco,* is well described in Chaskin, p. 81. See also the etching of "El Perfecto Currutaco" in Díaz-Plaja, p. 144.

2. He often makes fun of Romantic excesses: see Agustín del Campo, "Sobre la *Marcela* de Bretón," *Berceo,* II (1947), 41-55. For two humorous references to the Manzanares, see F. Navarro Villoslada, *Obras completas* (Madrid, 1947), p. 5; and the poem of Luis de Góngora, "El Río Manzanares," in his *Obras completas,* 3ª ed. (Madrid, 1951).

3. *Marcela* might be likened to Benavente's *Los intereses creados,* where the characters are puppets "who have meditated a lot in the last four hundred years." Buffoonery as in the *commedia dell' arte,* but not sheer buffoonery.

4. In the remainder of his note, Bretón confesses he sometimes had gone too far in experimenting with rhyme schemes, especially in his use of *esdrújulos.*

5. The Spanish language is by nature *llana,* that is, it tends to stress the penultimate syllable of a line. The *esdrújulo,* with its stress on the antepenult, is apt to be comical or altogether displeasing if repeated frequently.

6. The assonant rhyme in *ú* is a tour de force. See Chaskin, pp. 69-70; and Le Gentil, pp. 226-27.

7. Bretón himself has underscored the topic sentence of this play in an article to be found in his *Obra dispersa,* I, 172. And see Luisa Iravedra, "Las figuras femeninas del teatro de Bretón," *Berceo,* II (1947), 17-24.

8. The following critics, whose names appear in the end bibliography, have written at length on *Marcela:* Chaskin, Corey, Campo, Hesse, Iravedra, Le Gentil, and Molín.

9. Mariano José de Larra, *Artículos de crítica literaria y artística* (Madrid, 1950), pp. 125-26. This is vol. 52 of *Clásicos Castellanos.*

10. Larra, *Artículos de crítica literaria,* p. 100. See also *Obra dispersa,* I, 468.

11. Prior to reading Le Gentil, I myself had seen a likeness between Bretón and Balzac. For a different opinion, see Corey, p. 18. Chaskin, p. 78, citing Gil y Zárate, likens Bretón to Balzac in his portraits of women.

12. See Díaz-Plaja, where this and similar passages from Bretón are quoted.

13. Amado Nervo, *Obras completas* (Madrid, 1967), I, 476-77.

14. The principal difference between *A Sweetheart for the Girl* and the *alta comedia* is the latter's concentration on the *haute bourgeoisie.*

15. *A Sweetheart for the Girl* resembles Tamayo's *Lo positivo* (1862), López de Ayala's *Consuelo* (1878), Émile Augier's *Olympe's Marriage,* Victorien Sardou's *A Scrap of Paper,* and in English literature, the well-made plays of Henry Arthur Jones and Arthur Wing Pinero. See *Camille and Other Plays,* "edited with an introduction to the well-made play," by Stephen S. Stanton (New York, 1957): the Shavian remark appears on p. xxii.

16. I have purposely used Pereda as my reference here rather than some other source, of which there are many. Chapters XIV to XVI of *Pedro Sánchez* discuss many things pertinent to the present book; the fictitious Pedro even meets Bretón: "And he showed me a man, already mature, stocky, a commoner, a sort of very comfortable majordomo, and to top it all, one-eyed" (chapter XVI). José Maria de Pereda, *Pedro Sanchez,* dos tomos (Madrid: Espasa-Calpe, 1958); see vol. I, p. 159.

17. Curiously enough, the famous actor Julián Romea wrote ninety-six verses for the album of Bretón's own wife. See his "Romance escrito para el álbum de la Sra. Doña Tomasa Andrés de Bretón de los Herreros," in *Poesías de D. Julián Romea* (Sevilla, 1861), pp. 222-25.

18. See *Obras 1883,* V, where many of the poems resemble Juvenal's satires. And see Gilbert Highet, *Juvenal the Satirist* (Oxford, 1954), p. 41.

Bretón is scarcely as furious as Juvenal, although he imitates his fury.

19. I translate *fiel cristiana* as "a good young maid," although given the context of "Pelayo's god," it might admit a more literal translation.

20. See e.g., Galdós's novel *Miau,* whose principal character is Villa-amil, the *cesante.*

21. Although a *Marcela*-like play, *El cuarto de hora* is not as simple and unified as its "twin sister." Bretón provides for its more diverse action by dividing it into five acts rather than three.

22. The question of public favor is discussed by Cándido Bretón, Bretón's nephew, in *Obras 1883,* I, xi.

Chapter Six

1. The *Parnasillo* is described by Ramón de Mesonero Romanos in his *Obras,* V (Madrid, 1967), 173-76.

2. See Le Gentil, p. 30.

3. Ibid., p. 31.

4. Two Marivaux translations by Bretón are listed in *Obras 1883,* I, xxi. For the *marivaudage,* see O. Mandel, *Seven Comedies by Marivaux* (Ithaca, 1968), p. 5.

5. See Joseph Addison, "Sunday In The Country," in *A Book of English Essays,* ed. by W.E. Williams (London: Penguin Books, 1970), p. 44.

6. See Bretón's translation of Marivaux, *Engañar con la verdad,* pp. 144, 147, 161, 205; his translation of Scribe, *La familia del boticario* (*Obras 1850,* I, 270); and his translation of Monvel, *El regañón enamorado,* p. 188. See also Tirso de Molina's *Don Gil de las calzas verdes,* where I count a score of references to *talle;* Tirso's *El amor médico,* eight references; Rojas Zorrilla's *Entre bobos anda el juego,* four references; Moratín's *El sí de las niñas,* two references; and Bretón's *refundición* of Lope's *¡Si no vieran las mujeres!,* pp. 575, 578, 580, 585.

7. For a few of the many references to *talle* in Bretón, see: *La redacción de un periódico,* Act II, scene iii, and Act III, scene viii; *A Madrid me vuelvo,* Act I, scene iv; *Obra dispersa,* p. 208; *Obras 1883,* V, 136, 151, 221, 228, 262 (p. 136 shows *talle* as the source of poetry); *Los sentidos corporales,* Act I, scene vii; *Obras 1842,* I, 144, 147, 161, 205; *Mocedades,* Act III, scene iii, and Act I, scene iii; *Un tercero en discordia,* Act I, scene iii, and Act III, scene i; *La cabra tira al monte,* Act III, scene xv; *La niña del mostrador,* Act II, scene vi; *La batelera de Pasajes,* Act I, scene v; *Los solitarios,* Act I, scene xvii; *Entre santa y santo,* Act I, scene i; and *Los dos sobrinos,* Act I, scene vii. See also Fernando Calderón, who imitated Bretón's theater in Mexico, *A ninguna de las tres* (a word-play on *Marcela ¿a cuál de los tres?*), Act 1, scenes i and vii, Act II, scene ii. and see Moratín, *La mojigata,* Act I, scene vi, and *El sí de las niñas,* Act II, scene v.

8. Sebastián de Covarrubias, *Tesoro de la lengua,* edición preparada por Martín de Riquer (Barcelona: S.A. Horta, 1943), p. 952.

9. Bretón's vision of love is the same as Cervantes'. In the latter's novels a young man is on fire (Recaredo ardía); two girls are presented to him, the one virtuous, the other lascivious. The young man on fire should choose the virtuous beauty and marry her.

10. The psychiatrist Karl Stern sees this kind of love in the relation of Dante and Beatrice, and in Regina Olsen's love for Kierkegaard: "There was an immediate experience of recognition...." See K. Stern, *The Flight From Woman* (New York: Farrar, 1965), p. 218. One might say that in her instantaneous love for Kierkegaard, Regina Olsen met her *cuarto de hora.*

11. If the reader will examine the two love scenes of Cándido and Catalina, in Act II, scene iii, and Act III, scene ix, of *The Two Nephews,* he will see the development of the ideas expressed in this chapter: "Pero en fin llegó la hora:" Catalina has experienced her fateful moment.

12. Speaking of Turgeniev's *The Torrents of Spring,* Karl Stern writes: "Here, in the initial encounter with the young Italian girl, we have the Beatrice experience pure and simple — that sense of recognition, as though with some mysterious foreknowledge which is characteristic of all love" (p. 166). *Talle* and the model a girl carries in her fantasy lead to a mutual recognition.

13. Somewhere I have read, perhaps in George Meredith (I cannot find the reference in my notes), of a *fieffée coquette,* an arrant coquette, which is what Bretón means here. Later in the century Luis Coloma was to speak of "la frívola coquetería" and "la coquetería francesa." See Coloma, *Obras completas* (Madrid: Razón y Fe, 1960), pp. 1400, 1407.

14. Reprinted in *Obras 1883,* I, lix, and quoted by Chaskin, p. 87; and by Iravedra, p. 17. See also Bretón's play *Power of Attorney (Por poderes),* where Laura explicitly says there are two kinds of coquetry.

15. "Mira una y se hace mirar": this is the main thought of Lope de Vega's *¡Si no vieran las mujeres!,* which Bretón had adapted for the nineteenth century stage.

16. Molíns, discussing this passage in Chapter XXXVI of his book, praises its portrayal "of characters and customs." In Don Tadeo's speech, Bretón satirizes the use of a new word, *notabilidad,* recently acquired from the French.

17. Inglis, *Spain,* I, 224-25.

18. Luisa Iravedra writes: "Instead of the soft obedient line of the feminine figures conceived by his nearest model, Moratín, the female characters of Bretón have so much ease of manner and outgoingness [*desenvoltura y desembarazo*] that they may be compared to some of the women of our classical theater" (p. 17).

19. *Comedia* here means the seventeenth century theater.

20. See Bretón's "Discurso de acción de gracias a la Real Academia Española," *El liceo artístico y literario español* (1838), p. 112.

21. For more references to *galantería,* see *The School of Wives (La escuela de las casadas),* Act II, scene viii; Charles de Mazade, "La comédie moderne en Espagne," *Revue des Deux Mondes,* Paris, XIX (1847), 437; and Bretón's translation of Scribe's play, *El segundo año,* in *Obras 1850,* I, 279-92. In scene xvi of the Scribe play, a husband and wife discuss *galanterías* and *coqueterías.* The question of coquetry and gallantry had appeared in a play called *Coquetismo y presunción,* in May of 1831. Bretón so criticized the author, Francisco Flores Arenas, that a polemic ensued: see *Obra dispersa,* I, 54-56, 72-74.

22. The phrase "amorous carousel" is Larra's, in his review of Bretón's *Love's Referee (Un tercero en discordia).* Le Gentil, p. 142, adopts the phrase, "carrousel amoureux."

23. I have in my notes many references to marriage as well as to *talle, coquetería* and *galantería.* See, for example, Bretón's translation of Scribe in *Obras 1850,* I, 304; his own one act *My Secretary and I (Mi secretario y yo),* scene iii; and *Her Fateful Moment (El cuarto de hora),* Act II, scene i.

24. Concerning *desenvoltura,* see Ramón Menéndez Pidal, "El lenguaje del siglo XVI," in *La lengua de Cristobal Colón,* 4a. ed. (Madrid, 1958), p. 58; and see Fray Juan de los Angeles, *Manual de vida perfecta,* Diálogo 5, p. 619, in *Místicos franciscanos españoles,* III (Madrid, 1949): his *afable* is the *desenvoltura* of Cervantes's little gypsy girl (See Cervantes, *The Little Gypsy,* in *The Deceitful Marriage and Other Exemplary Novels,* Trans. by Walter Starkie (New York, 1963), p. 57. See also Act II, scene vii, of Bretón's *The Girl at the Counter (La niña del mostrador),* where the young girl resembles Preciosa, *la gitanilla.* Le Gentil, pp. 196, 210, 226, 228, 231, and Mazade, p. 446, both comment on *désinvolture* and *souplesse.* See also Campo, 41-55.

25. In Cervantes's *El casamiento engañoso,* the ensign Campuzano marries a loose woman who gives him a venereal disease. See Miguel de Cervantes, *The Deceitful Marriage and Other Exemplary Novels,* Translated by Walter Starkie (New York, 1963), p. 92.

26. See Alonso Cortés, p. xiv.

27. See Marcelino Menéndez Playo, *Antología general de Menéndez Pelayo* (Madrid, 1956), p. 945.

28. Martínez Villergas, p. 25. On p. 37 Martínez Villergas defends Bretón against his enemies, although earlier in his career he had attacked him: see Alonso Cortés, pp. xiii, xxi.

29. This may be Cervantes's point of view in the *Quixote* itself. The interpolated "Tale of Foolish Curiosity" ends with the idea that, the content aside, a story is worthwhile provided it is told well. And see Somerset Maugham, *The Writer's Point of View* (London, 1951), p. 7.

30. Spanish critics have often used the phrase *fondo y forma.* I am translating *fondo* as *subject,* because the nineteenth century critics were in effect arguing: if Bretón had treated more profound subjects he would have written better plays.

31. His theater is, moreover, a rather faithful historical record of the manners of the time; recall this quotation from the English traveler, Inglis: "Every Spanish house has its *tertulia*... Gallantry is the business of every Spaniard's life" (pp. 224-25). Thus, the subject of Bretón's theater is from this viewpoint the activity of "every Spanish house" and the business of every Spaniard. Bretón's plays were also accused of superficial characterization. It would be fruitful to pursue this question further, since several drama critics give characterization a secondary place in comedy; e.g., "In tragedy the plot dances to the tune of the characters, in comedy the characters dance to the tune of the plot" (Calderwood and Toliver, pp. 172-73). See also Ramón Pérez de Ayala, "Comicidad Inteligente," in *Amistades y Recuerdos* (Barcelona, 1961), pp. 274-78.

Juan Donoso Cortés's famous essay, "El clasicismo y el romanticismo," will show how both classicists and romantics might consider Bretón's plays superficial. For the classicists, Bretón wrote about humble people rather than "magnates and heroes." For the romantics, he "was never inspired by the groans which are wrenched from the heart of men or from the entrails of nations." When Bretón wrote historical dramas about magnates and heroes, such as the romantic work, *Elena,* he was apparently trying to please both parties! Donoso Cortés takes a middle road between dogmatic classicism and dogmatic romanticism: "Then perfection consists in being classic and romantic at the same time...." Donoso Cortés, *Obras completas* (Madrid, 1946), I, 381-409; see especially pp. 381-82.

Concerning the question of superficiality, see also Mazade, pp. 445-47; Hartzenbusch's prologue to the *Obras 1883,* I, lvi; and Brunetière, pp. 66-133.

Chapter Seven

1. See Chapter Six, note 26.

2. So states the Marqués de Molíns, as quoted by Julio Cejador y Frauca, *Historia de la lengua y literatura castellana* (Madrid, 1918), VI, 410-11. See also Molíns, pp. 218-19.

3. Cejador y Frauca uses the expression *coronarlo.* The audience had done the same for Antonio García Gutiérrez on the first showing of *El Trovador,* March 1836.

4. Hartzenbusch, *Obras 1883,* I, lv; and as quoted in Le Gentil, p. 37.

5. Chaskin, pp. 127, 131.

6. Molíns, pp. 209-210; Le Gentil, p. 83. See also Adelaide Parker and E. Allison Peers in the following articles: "The Vogue of Victor Hugo in Spain," *Modern Language Review,* XXVII (1932), 36-57; "The Influence of Victor Hugo on Spanish Poetry and Prose Fiction," *Modern Language Review,* XXVIII (1933), 50-61; and "The Influence of Victor Hugo on Drama," *Modern Language Review,* XXVIII (1933), 205-16.

7. *Obras 1883,* IV, 151-52.

Notes and References

8. A servant, Ramón, and an offstage notary also know of his return.

9. See, for example, Zorrilla's legend of *El capitán Montoya,* and Espronceda's *El estudiante de Salamanca.* See also Lewis E. Brett, *Nineteenth Century Spanish Plays* (New York, 1935), pp. 285-86.

10. See Corey, pp. 135-41.

11. *Economizar* was also the favorite word of Torquemada, the miser in Galdós's *Torquemada en la Cruz.*

12. If Elías were conscious of his vice we could scarcely laugh at him; a miser conscious of his miserliness would be a tragic figure or at least a dramatic one.

13. Molière "never inveighed against those vices which were instinctive and conformable to nature." His targets were "all those who disguise nature..." (Brunetière, pp. 71-72).

14. In French, as in Spanish, *juif* may mean "Usurier, homme âpre au gain," as well as "Jew" or "Jewish": thus a Lombard or Genoese moneylender might be called a *juif.* Mazade's statement (p. 447) is not as explicit as Corcy's (p. 140).

15. Perhaps Bretón had not only seen selfish antipatriots but had also recalled Feijoo's essay, "Amor de la patria y pasión nacional," which begins: "I look for in men that love of country which I find so praised in books; ... and I do not find it." See Fray B.J. Feijoo, *Ensayos escogidos* (Madrid, 1944).

16. See V.A. Chamberlin, "Galdós's Use of Yellow in Character Delineation," *PMLA,* 79 (1964), 158-63.

17. See Brunetière, pp. 71-72.

18. For the *barbero* as a *tipo,* see José F. Montesinos, *Costumbrismo y novela,* 2ª ed. (Madrid, 1960), p. 65.

19. Chaskin, pp. 127-33.

20. Pablo is a lieutenant, Matías a sublieutenant. I picture the latter as shorter, darker, more devious, and more selfish.

21. For a simple exposition of Spanish prosody, see Hymen Alpern and José Martel, *Diez comedias del siglo de oro* (New York, 1939), pp. xxv-xxviii; and also Rafael Lapesa, *Introducción a los estudios literarios* (Madrid, 1968), chs. IX-XIV.

22. The phrase is Shlegel's, who borrows it from N. Adam Müller. See A.W. Schlegel, *Course of Lectures on Dramatic Art and Literature* (London, 1846; New York: AMS Press, 1965), p. 341.

23. See Brett, p. 285.

24. See Chaskin, pp. 127-32; Brett, p. 169; and Angel Valbuena Prat, *Historia de la literatura española* (Barcelona, 1960), III, 231.

25. *Manolo* is perhaps the most famous *sainete* of the Spanish language. Of a lesser order, Muñoz Seca's play is famous for its total caricature of Romantic interpretations of classical Spanish theater.

26. See José Francisco Gatti, *Ramón de la Cruz, Doce Sainetes* (Barcelona, 1972), pp. 18-20.

27. See *Obras 1883,* I, lv.
28. P. Francisco Blanco García, *La literatura española en el siglo XIX,* 3ª ed., parte primera (Madrid, 1909), p. 282.
29. See Alonso Cortés', p. xxviii. Since Romantic theater is ordinarily associated with dramas, this statement about a *comedia romántica* may be the reconciling criticism.
30. The stage directions indicate twelve characters by name, and "a blind man, blind woman, national guardsmen, men and women in mourning, ladies and gentlement guests, the people." Thus some scenes present fifty or more people on the stage; compare this with Moratín's seven characters or *Marcela's* six. Nevertheless, the plot is similar: Pablo must choose a wife, Jacinta the coquette or Isabel the modest lady. The suggestion of a Romantic comedy, as distinct from Romantic tragedy, squares with the findings of a recent article, "The Romantic Element in Bretón's *Muérete ¡y verás!"* (Allen, pp. 218-27).

Muérete resembles Regnard's *Le Légataire universel* and *Molière's Le Malade imaginaire:* see W.A. Nitze and E.P. Dargan, *A History of French Literature,* 3rd ed. (New York, 1938), p. 424.
31. See Le Gentil, pp. 37, 278.
32. See Pío Baroja, *El árbol de la ciencia,* ed. by Gerard Flynn (New York, 1970), Quinta Parte, Capítulo II.
33. The *Obras* of 1850 and 1883 give the date of the premiere as February 13, but apparently the true opening date was February 19. See Alonso Cortés, pp. xxviii, xxix.
34. See José Simón Díaz, "Nuevas fuentas para el estudio de Bretón," *Berceo,* II (1947), 40. The premiere was given as a benefit for Lombía: see Alonso Cortés, p. xxviii.
35. Cariñena, a town some twenty-eight miles southwest of Zaragoza, also appears in *Die and You Shall See!*
36. A *quintal* is forty-six kilograms, or one hundred pounds. Perhaps Frutos had a lesser *quintal* in mind.
37. Fernando Díaz-Plaja writes: "Until well into the century it can be affirmed that elegance consisted in being form-fitted (*ceñido*) pp. 79-80).".
38. The subject of impecunious nobility's marrying wealth also appears in Bretón's *In Arrears (Cuentas atrasadas)* (1841) and *My Secretary and I (Mi secretario y yo)* (1841). See also Azorín's essay on *The Country Bumpkin* in *Ante las Candilejas-Costumbres,* in his *Obras completas* (Madrid, 1954), IX, 74-76.
39. His full name is Don Frutos Calamocha y Centeno, which translates literally as Don Fruit of Red Earth and Rye. Moratín has a humorous servant, Calamocha, in *El sí de las niñas.*
40. The definition of the Dictionary of the Royal Spanish Academy.
41. See Valbuena Prat, III, 233.
42. Don Juan Valera used this phrase to characterize Bretón's theater (II, 1272-77).

Notes and References

43. See e.g., the discreet verses of Isabel and Pedro in Rojas Zorrilla's *Entre bobos anda el juego,* vv. 79-889, vv. 981-1110, and vv. 1205-1302, and compare them with Frutos's *a la pata la llana* verses in Act IV, scene viii, and Act II, scene xi.
44. See Germán Bleiberg, *Diccionario de literatura española,* 3ª ed. (Madrid, 1964), p. 695.
45. Silvia Novo Chaskin sees a likeness between Don Frutos and Larra's *El castellano viejo* and argues that in *The Country Bumpkin* Bretón was showing the effect of the new customs on a traditional Spaniard, p. 170. See also Le Gentil, p. 281; and Villergas, pp. 21-25.
46. See Le Gentil, p. 197: "L'accent aragonais fait l'intérêt principal de *Don Frutos en Belchite.*"
47. A footnote reads: "This is a proverbial phrase in a large part of Aragon" (viz., "¡De Belchite, y lloras!": "You cry, and you're from Belchite! — *Obras 1883,* II, 369).
48. *Obras 1883,* V, 89-94. This *Satire* is addressed to Molíns.
49. See Valera, II, 1272-77, for an account of the profound changes occurring in Spain and their relation to Bretón's theater.
50. See Le Gentil, pp. 287-88.
51. Hugo, *Alpes et Pyrénées. Pasages,* as quoted by Le Gentil, p. 288.
52. She has reached her *cuarto de hora,* her fateful moment; see Chapters 4 and 5, above.
53. The word *lo* refers to *poeta* of the preceding line not here quoted.
54. I wrote the word *net* spontaneously and on first reflection thought it was an unfortunate pun, since Faustina comes from a fishermen's town. But the captain himself has said: "La Herrera / que cría entre sus peces / tan linda batelera." He is the hunter, or fisherman, and she his prey.
55. The civil war of 1833-1839 was still raging in northern Spain at the time the play takes place, and Captain Bureba has been commissioned to visit Commodore John Hay, chief of the English auxiliary squadron. See *Obras 1883,* III, 86.
56. See Ramón Menéndez Pidal, *Flor nueva de romances viejos* (Buenos Aires, 1963), p. 24. This book contains the ballad "La Mora Moraima," pp. 209-210.
57. Manuel Tamayo y Baus makes the same division in *La ricahembra* (1854), where Act I is taken from a Spanish ballad, and Acts II, III, and IV are really a separate play. Apparently Lope de Vega's three act formula for the spanish *comedia* was not easily broken.
58. One can liken the Pasajes scene to the poetical theater of Federico García Lorca: the rustic scene, the chorus, the *aldeanas,* the quality of the verses, the intelligent use of spectacle and even ballet.
59. In the play, Pablo writes a letter dated April 24, 1839. This is just four months before the Agreement of Vergara (August 29-31, 1839), ending the seven year Carlist war.
60. *Sagardúa,* cider in Vizcaya; *chacolí,* a light red wine made in

Vizcaya; *aguardiente de guindas,* Mazard brandy; *sardinas,* sardines. Such was the fare of a canteen.

61. *El Independiente,* January 19, 1843: as quoted in Molíns, p. 309.
62. Piñeyro, p. 211.
63. Blanco García, p. 287.
64. Brunetière, p. 66. Molíns likens *The Ferry-Girl From Pasajes* to Calderón's *El Alcalde de Zalamea,* and many critics have repeated his argument. See Molíns, pp. 309-20.

Chapter Eight

1. Valera, II, 1273-74.
2. *Obras 1883,* I, 189.
3. This apt phrase is Sean O'Faolain's, in *The Short Story* (New York, 1951), p. 74. O'Faolain's chapter on Alphonse Daudet might profitably be applied to Bretón: "Daudet was the local boy who made good; *le petit chose* who became *grande chose.*" But, O'Faolain says, his books are readable for their "Daudet-ism" not their "Zola-ism." Similarly, Bretón's theater is memorable for its Bretón-ism not its serious-drama-ism. "No subject is too small for genius" (O'Faolain, p. 74).
4. I should like to include the following plays in this category: *Reality and Appearance (Lo vivo y lo pintado),* 1841; *Birds of a Feather (La cabra tira al monte),* 1853; *Independence (La independencia),* 1844; *The Girl at the Counter (La niña del mostrador),* 1854; *The School of Matrimony (La escuela del matrimonio),* 1852; and *The Worthy Woman (El valor de la mujer),* 1852. Bretón made his own list of works he considered dramas in his footnote to *Show Me the Woman (¿Quién es ella?),* viz., *Elena, Don Fernando the Summoned (Don Fernando el Emplazado), She Is He (Ella es él), Treat Disdain With Love (Finezas contra desvíos), Die and You Shall See!, Her Fateful Moment (El cuarto de hora), Independence (La independencia),* and *The Ferry-Girl from Pasajes.*
5. These ideas appear in Tamayo's Academy speech: see Flynn, pp. 97-109.
6. See Donoso Cortés, I, 381-409.
7. The distinguished Hispanist José F. Montesinos takes a dim view of Mesonero in his *Costumbrismo y novela* See Ramón Mesonero Romanos, *Selections,* ed. by George Tyler Northup (New York: Henry Holt, 1913), pp. 51-56.
8. Bretón also satirizes Romanticism in *The Poet and the Actress (El poeta y la beneficiada),* "fábula cómica en dos actos," 1838. See also Le Gentil, pp. 35, 119; Corey, pp. 141, 143, and César Barja, *Libros y autores modernos* (Los Angeles, 1933), pp. 141-43, 220.
9. Concerning banditry, see Wallis, pp. 316-18.
10. Martínez Villergas, p. 32, says that both plays were "only moderate successes."

11. See Molíns, pp. 140–43; and also Le Gentil, pp. 100–101.
12. See Adelaide Parker and E.A. Peers, "The Influence of Victor Hugo on Spanish Drama," *Modern Language Review*, XXVIII (1933), 205–16.
13. Bretón was also influenced by Tirso de Molina's *La prudencia en la mujer*, which concerns the regency of Doña María de Molina during the minority of Fernando IV, the *emplazado*. Tirso's *comedia* ends with mention of a second play by him, *The Two Carvajales*, as if he were foretelling the plot of Bretón's *Don Fernando The Summoned*.
14. Juan Cortada, *Historia de España desde los tiempos más remotos hasta 1839* (Barcelona, 1841), pp. 73–74. Note that Bretón's play came out in 1837 and this history in 1841; the latter is rather like a condensation of the former: the climate is the same. See also Antonio Benavides, *Memorias de D. Fernando IV de Castilla*, I (Madrid, 1860), 691–96.
15. Apparently the audiences of Bretón's day found them ponderous also: see John A. Cook, *Neo-Classic Drama in Spain* (Dallas, 1959), p. 502.
16. *No ganamos para sustos* is construed to mean "no podemos estar tranquilos un instante," in Bretón, *La independencia*, edited by James Geddes et al. (New York, 1924), p. 220.
17. For the historical background of the play, see Henry Kamen, *The War of Succession in Spain, 1700–1715* (Bloomington, 1969), pp. 20–23.
18. The *Obra dispersa* includes Bretón's articles in the *Correo Literario* from 1831 to 1833.
19. Molíns, p. 308, calls it "frankly and clearly an imitation of the *comedia de capa y espada*."
20. Bretón calls him "el Juvenal español" in his long poem, "A Quevedo"; see *Obras 1883*, V, 304.
21. In his necrology in *La Ilustración Española y Americana*, XVII, xlv (1873), pp. 727–30, Ramón de Navarrete says that "There was a period when the critics, who were enamored of other younger authors, declared war to the death against the compositions of Bretón.... This explains the mystery of how he staged the drama ¿*Quién es ella?*, which excited so much the curiosity of the public and which won him a signal triumph." See also Wallis, pp. 210–13; and W.F. Smith, "Rodríguez Rubí and the Dramatic Reforms of 1849," *Hispanic Review*, XVI (1948), 319–20.
22. *H* is probably Hartzenbusch; *V*, Vega; and *R*, Rodríguez Rubí, although it might be Rivas.
23. The note was written later in life, for the posthumous edition of his works. See the statement of his nephew, Cándido Bretón, in *Obras 1883*, I, lxii.
24. See the third person *yoísmo* of Unamuno in his letters to Clarín, in *Epistolario a Clarín*, prólogo y notas de Adolfo Alas (Madrid, 1941), pp. 53–54.
25. See the quotation of Juan Martínez Villergas, in Chapter 6, above;

and see also note 27 there, which will bear out this statement. Martínez Villergas, p. 13, claims that he and others saw through Bretón's *incognito.* See also Molíns, p. 474, whose words suggest that Bretín was writing under duress.

Chapter Nine

1. Molíns, pp. 264-65.
2. See Ibid., p. 267. On March 16, 1838, Bretón wrote to Molíns: "Aplaude V. que me dedique a estos juguetes dramáticos, siguiendo el sistema de Scribe" (Ibid., pp. 264-65). Thus, some of the one act plays are admittedly Scribian.
3. Concerning Horace's *dulcis et utile,* and its Spanish equivalent, *enseñar deleitando,* see E.C. Riley, *Cervantes's Theory of the Novel* (Oxford, 1962), pp. 81-88.
4. Translating French *comediejas,* as he calls them, constituted his apprenticeship in this genre; of the twenty-seven, eleven were by Scribe.
5. Bretón also wrote seven circumstantial plays; e.g., on Ferdinand VII's marriage; on his return to court; on the defense of Bilbao against the Carlists; on the opening of the Ebro River to navigation. Thus Bretón had some of the duties of a poet laureate.
6. *figurón* is a person cutting a ridiculous appearance. The first known *comedia de figurón* was Rojas Zorrilla's *Entre bobos anda el juego* (1638).
7. The reader interested in the question of French vaudeville and Spanish theater should read MM. Felix August Duvert, Desvergers, and Varin, *La Famille de l'Apothicaire ou La Petite Prude* (Paris, 1830), and Bretón's translation of it, *La familia del boticario* (1832). In a footnote to this translation, Bretón writes: "When he [Bretón] translated this play, the author successfully tried to preserve in the translation some of the popular songs that abound in French *vaudevilles,* although in that nation the actors sing them, whereas in ours they limit themselves to reciting them. He did the same thing in other works of the same origin, and he followed this practice once again in his original comedy, *The Fat Man.*" See *Obras 1850,* I, 269.
8. *One More Coquette* is the only one of Bretón's plays translated into English. See Willis Knapp Jones and Hayward Keniston, *Spanish One-Act Plays in English,* which renders the title as *One of Many* (Dallas: Tardy Publishing Co., 1934), pp. 176-97.
9. The expression is used in scene xiv: "¿Vienes tal vez de pelar la pava?" Bretón wrote an *artículo de costumbres,* "Pelar la pava," which appears in Le Gentil, pp. 522-23. See also Ibid., pp. 14, 129, 250.
10. Henry David Inglis, *A Lecture Upon The Truth . . . of Phrenology,* 2nd ed. (London, 1826), p. 3. A well-written essay on the doctrines of Gall and Spurzheim. The Spanish emigres were in London at this time, and one of them, Mateo Seoane, published an essay there in 1825 on phrenology.

Notes and References   155

See Vicente Lloréns, *Liberales y románticos* (Madrid, 1968), p. 177: Lloréns refers to Bretón's play.

11. See the works of Mariano Cubí y Soler (1801-1875). Bretón's footnote reads: "The presence in this city of the famous phrenologist and hypnotizer, Cubí, and his experiments and readings in both subjects put them in vogue for a while; and, as often happens in such cases, there was no lack of daring and ignorant amateurs who began to practice one skill or the other, right and left. This abuse is what the author proposed to ridicule in the present comic story; and not any specific person; nor the above said arts or sciences, whichever they might be; for he does not consider himself a competent judge either to praise them or attack them" (*Obras 1883*, II, 441).

12. The *Dictionary of the Royal Academy* explains the proverb in terms of moral theology: for a man and woman to be closeted alone is a "proximate occasion" of sin.

13. "Eloquent proverb:" see Bretón's own footnote in *Obras 1883*, IV, 459.

14. For Bretón's footnote to *Entre santa y santo*, see *Obras 1883*, IV, 459. Among other things, he says: "There are no intrigues, no perfidious ties. Without design, and even against their will, the three find themselves occupying the seats, by no means comfortable, of the berlin in a diligence." Bretón himself recognized the greatness of this piece in its simplicity. The love of Modesto and Engracia is cut of the same cloth as Gabriel's love for Inés in Galdós's *National Episodes*.

Chapter Ten

1. See *Obra dispersa*, p. 5.
2. See E. Correa Calderón, *Costumbristas españoles*, 2ª ed. (Madrid, 1964), I, 1014-1339. Two humorous stories worth preserving are the "Ici on se tutoie," anecdote in *Obras 1850*, V, 614, and the Dido anecdote in *Obras 1850*, V, 607.
3. Molíns, p. 163.
4. Le Gentil, pp. 235-36 and pp. 249-61.
5. For example, Alonso de Castillo Solórzano (1584-1648) wrote an *entremés*, *La Castañera*.
6. A reference to Manuel Godoy, who did not die until 1851.
7. The 'broad hints of *Padre Cobos*' does not refer to the satirical journal, *El Padre Cobos*, which did not appear until 1854, but to an older tradition. See Le Gentil, p. 255, note 2.
7. See *Obra dispersa*, p. 5.
9. This is according to private correspondence I have received from the Instituto de Estudios Riojanos, which published the *Obra dispersa*.
10. For a comparison of Bretón's criticism with Larra's, see *Obra dispersa*, pp. 28-29.

11. A newspaper at that time consisted of four sheets.
12. I am aware of no other edition of this work. The *Declamación* runs thirty-four double column pages of small print, or about one hundred fifty pages in a book of conventional size.
13. See *Obra dispersa*, pp. 217–18, before reading the *Declamación*.
14. Molíns mentions the *Resumen de Actas y Tareas*, saying they run from 1859 to 1868 (Molíns, p. 522).
15. The editors of the *Obra dispersa*, p. 5, also refer to Bretón's "speeches" and *Sinónimos castellanos*, which I have not read. See also Bretón's nephew, Cándido Bretón y Orozco, in *Obras 1883*, I, xlii.
16. See *Obras 1883*, V, 7. Bretón had to compose a poem each week for the *Abeja* and similar journals (*Obras 1883*, V, 174–75).
17. See *Obras 1883*, V, 7–8.
18. In his *Juicio crítico* Juan Marínez Villergas says: "Study him in his dialogues, not as a lyrical poet." (p. 15).
19. See Pedro Antonio de Alarcón's comments in *Obras completas* de Alarcón, 2ª ed. (Madrid, 1954), pp. 1782–85.
20. Some of the *romances* make an extreme use of antepenults (*esdrújulos*); see, e.g., the 288 verses of "Lamentos de un Poeta."
21. See Alarcón, p. 1785. Molíns, pp. 166–84 and 522–23, argues that some of Bretón's *letrillas* are "highly political."
22. The three daughters of a certain Dr. Vives, whom Bretón, Vega, Pezuela, and others courted as young men.
23. Wallis, p. 213.
24. Le Gentil, p. 232.
25. See Brander Matthews, *French Dramatists in the Nineteenth Century* (New York, 1901), p. 102. Concerning Scribe's influence, see also Le Gentil, pp. 75–88; Molíns, pp. 264–69; N.B. Adams, "Notes on Spanish Plays at the Beginning of the Romantic Period," *Romanic Review*, XVII (1926), 136–42; Martínez Villergas, pp. 7, 39; Bretón's *Obra dispersa*, passim.; N.B. Adams, *The Romantic Dramas of García Gutiérrez* (New York, 1922), pp. 54–59, 117; Díaz-Plaja, pp. 237–38; p. 334; Chaskin, pp. 64, 90; Cejador y Frauca, p. 407; Sterling Stoudemire, "Gil y Zárate's Translations of French Plays," *Modern Language Notes*, XLVIII (1933), p. 322; and Mariano José de Larra, "Una Primera Representación," in *Biblioteca de Autores Españoles* (Madrid, 1960), vol. 128, 68–73). One area of French theater has been virtually untouched by the critics in its relation to Spanish nineteenth century theater, namely, the French *vaudevilles*, or, *comédies-vaudevilles*. They seem to be an important key to the new Spanish *zarzuela* (e.g., Bretón calls his *zarzuela* "comedia-zarzuela," a contradiction in terms according to Emilio Cotarelo y Mori, *Historia de la zarzuela* [Madrid, 1934].)
26. I am publishing an article on the *refundiciones* of Bretón in the new journal, *Estudos Ibero-Americanos*. It should appear in 1978.
27. In answer to my letter, the Instituto de Estudios Riojanos has

Notes and References 157

advised me: "...you ask us if we know any heirs of Bretón de los Herreros. We know of none."

28. Northrop Frye speaks of demotion and promotion in literary criticism, e.g., "Demoting Shelley, on the ground that he is immature in technique and profundity of thought...." See N. Frye, *Anatomy of Criticism* (Princeton, 1957), p. 23.

29. See Cotarelo y Mori, pp. 151-67.

30. Such is the theory of Cotarelo y Mori, pp. 175-78, who declares that Larra and Bretón were unconscious of what they were doing.

31. At that time the word *melo-drama,* or music-drama, appears instead of *zarzuela.* For distinctions between the opera, *zarzuela,* and operetta, see Rafael Lapesa, *Introducción a los estudios literarios* (Salamanca, 1972), pp. 169-70.

32. Notice that Bretón dropped the three act *zarzuelas* from his collected works and kept the one act pieces; thus he foretells the tendency of the *zarzuela* toward the *género chico.*

33. See Alarcón, pp. 1817-24; also Augusto Martínez Olmedilla, *Anecdotario del siglo XIX* (Madrid, 1957), pp. 368-70, 411-15.

34. See the footnote to *Obras 1883,* II, 219.

35. José Zorrilla, *Recuerdos del tiempo viejo,* as quoted by Adams, "Notes on Spanish Plays," p. 130. See also the article "Pata de cabra" in the *Enciclopedia ilustrada* of Espasa-Calpe, vol. 42, p. 682.

36. See *Obra dispersa,* pp. 115-17, 334-35. *La pata de cabra* was first staged in 1828.

37. See *Obras 1883,* I, lxiii.

38. Bretón's *Joco el orangután* of 1831 may not be original, for a play of the same name appeared in France and England in 1825. See Alardyce Nicoll, *A History of Early Nineteenth-Century Drama, 1800-1850,* I (Cambridge, 1930), 26.

39. Concerning the magic play, see also Ramón de Mesonero Romanos, *Obras,* in the *Biblioteca de Autores Españoles* (Madrid, 1967), vol. 203, 179; and John Kenneth Leslie, *Ventura de la Vega* (Princeton, 1940), pp. 30, 85

40. The passages celebrating taste and touch are plays on words, and less lyrical. But see Molíns, p. 507.

41. Bretón did not include *The Bodily Senses* in his collected works, and he tells why in *Obras 1883,* I, lxiii. See also Piñeyro, p. 218; and Molíns, pp. 505-13.

42. These are the opinions of Ernest Merimée and Boris de Tannenberg, as cited in Le Gentil, p. 515.

43. See Poyán Díaz, II, 58-81.

44. Again, the pun concerning Bretón's loss of his left eye is accidental, but perhaps not unfortunate. He himself would joke about his wound.

45. This facetious remark, which I heard twenty years ago in graduate school, sums up the attitude of many Hispanists toward the nineteenth century theater.

46. Bretón may have been, subconsciously, a Spanish surrogate for Balzac and Molière. French critics have compared him to the former, and with respect to the latter, Bretón even wrote an original play called *The School for Wives* (premiere, May 3, 1842, in verse.)
46. Mazade, p. 447.
48. Le Gentil, p. 199.
49. Horace, as quoted in *Obras 1883,* V, 17.
50. Modesto Lafuente, *Teatro social del siglo XIX por Fray Gerundio,* 2 vols. (Madrid, 1846). See the title page of Lafuente, whose humorous articles often resemble the plays of Bretón.
51. Dámaso Alonso, *La poesía de San Juan de la Cruz* (Madrid, 1958), p. 74.

Selected Bibliography

The journal *Estudos Ibero-Americanos,* 1:2 (Dezembro de 1975), 299-317, has published my article "An Annotated Bibliography of Manuel Bretón de los Herreros," in which there are many more secondary sources and a description of each one of the primary sources. The present *Selected Bibliography* is a reduction of that article.

PRIMARY SOURCES

1. Editions of Bretón's works. Collections, in chronological order.

Teatro. 6 vols. Ed. José María Lafragua. México: Imprenta de Vicente García Torres, 1842-1843.
Obras. 5 vols. Madrid: Imprenta Nacional, 1850-1851.
Obras escogidas. 2 vols. Paris: Baudry, 1853.
Obras. 5 vols. Madrid: Imprenta de Miguel Ginesta, 1883-1884.
Teatro. Prólogo y notas de Narciso Alonso Cortés. In *Clásicos Castellanos,* vol. 92. Madrid: Espasa-Calpe, 1943.
Obra dispersa. Tomo I. *El Correo Literario y Mercantil.* Edición y estudio de J.M. Díez Taboada y J.M. Rozas. Logroño: Instituto de Estudios Riojanos, Imprenta Moderna, 1965.
Obras teatrales: Marcela o ¿a cuál de los tres?; Muérete ¡y verás!; La escuela del matrimonio. Edición, prólogo y notas de Francisco Serrano Puente. Logroño: Instituto de Estudios Riojanos, 1975.

2. Editions of Bretón's Works. Single Plays and Other Works. All but five of the works listed below do not appear in the 1842, 1850, 1853, and 1883 collections of Bretón's plays.

A la vejez viruelas. Comedia original en tres actos. Madrid: Imprenta de Miguel de Burgos, 1825.
El amante prestado. Comedia en un acto. Madrid: Imprenta de Cipriano López, 1857.
Los carlistas en Portugal, o, La tremenda expedición. A one-act farce appearing in the newspaper *El Universal,* April 15, 1834, pp. 2-4.
Cosas de Don Juan. Zarzuela en tres actos. Música de Don Rafael Hernando. Madrid: Imprenta de C. González, 1854.
Desconfianza y travesura, o, A la zorra candilazo. Madrid: Imprenta de Cipriano López, 1857.
El Ebro. Comedia en un acto. Madrid: Imprenta Nacional, 1857.

Las improvisaciones. Madrid: Imprenta de los hijos de Doña Catalina Piñuela, 1837.
La Independencia. Edited by James Geddes, Grace E. Merrill, Bertha A. Merrill, and Joseph C. Palamountain. New York: Charles Scribner's, 1924.
La loca fingida. Drama en un acto. Madrid: Imprenta de Repullés, 1833.
Marcela, o ¿a cuál de los tres? Edición e introducción de José Hesse. Madrid: Taurus Ediciones, 1969.
Marcela, o ¿a cuál de los tres? Edited by William S. Hendrix. New York: Benjamin H. Sanborn Co., 1922.
Mi empleo y mi muger. Comedia en tres actos. Madrid: Imprenta de D. León Aminta, 1835.
Mocedades. Comedia en tres actos. Original y en verso. Madrid: Imprenta de José Rodríguez, 1857.
El novio pasado por agua, Zarzuela de figurón en tres actos. Música de Don Rafael Hernando. Madrid: C. González, 1852.
Otro diablo predicador, o, El liberal por fuerza. Madrid: Imprenta de Repullés, 1835.
El pelo de la dehesa. Edited by Joseph Manson; introduction by J.M. Blair. London: G. Bell, 1955.
El pelo de la dehesa. Edición de José Montero Padilla. Madrid: Ediciones Cátedra, 1974.
El plan de un drama, o, La conspiración. Madrid: Imprenta de Repullés, 1835.
Le poil de la prairie. Paris: Imprimerie de Boulé, 1847. The only French translation of a Bretón play I have seen; it is listed in the catalogue of the Bibliothèque Nationale in Paris.
La ponchada. Madrid: Imprenta de Yenes, 1840. Written in collaboration with the actor, Julián Romea.
¿Quién es ella? Comedia en cinco actos. Edited by Samuel Garner. New York: American Book Company, 1905.
Resumen de las actas y tareas de la Real Academia Española en el año académico de 1860 a 1861. Madrid: Imprenta Nacional, 1861. This was the yearly report Bretón read as executive secretary of the Royal Academy; there are also reports for the years 1862–1869.
Los sentidos corporales. Comedia en tres actos y en verso. Madrid: Imprenta de José Rodríguez, 1867.
El templo de Himeneo. Madrid: Imprenta de I. Sancha, 1829.

3. Special References

BRETÓN DE LOS HERREROS, MANUEL. "Literatura Dramática. De la utilidad de la versificación en los dramas." *El liceo artístico y literario español,* vol. II, 1838. This is Bretón's Academy speech of June 15, 1837, minus the exordium and with a "few slight changes." (See *Obras 1883,* I, xlii).

Los españoles pintados por sí mismos. Por varios autores. Madrid: Gaspar y Roig, Editores, 1851. Contains four *artículos de costumbres* by Bretón and other articles by several contemporaries.

BRETÓN DE LOS HERREROS, MANUEL. "Progresos y Estado Actual del Arte de la Declamación en los Teatros de España." *Obras escogidas,* I (Paris: Baudry, 1853). The first half of this book length essay is a history of the Spanish theater from Juan del Encina to the nineteenth century; the second half, a history of the actor's art, declamation.

OCHOA Y RONNA, EUGENIO. *Apuntes para una biblioteca de escritores contemporáneos,* I (Paris: Baudry, 1840). Pages 123-31 are Bretón's Academy entrance speech, a version of it to be compared with the first special reference above.

"Literatura Dramática. Reseña de un debate sostenido en el Liceo de Madrid." In *Revista literaria de El Español,* I (1846), 14-16. Bretón and other famous writers discuss the problem of whether authors of their day can successfully imitate the dramatic poets of the seventeenth century.

SECONDARY SOURCES

Scholarly Criticism and Interpretation

ADAMS, NICHOLSON B. "French Influence on the Madrid Theater in 1837." *Estudios dedicados a D. Ramón Menéndez Pidal,* pp. 135-51. Madrid: CSIC, Biblioteca Reyes, 1950.

———. "Notes on Dramatic Criticism in Madrid: 1828-1833." *Studies in Language and Literature,* pp. 231-38. Chapel Hill: University of North Carolina Press, 1945.

———. "Notes on Spanish Plays at the Beginning of the Romantic Period." *Romanic Review,* XVII (1926), 128-42.

———. "Sidelights on the Spanish Theaters of the Eighteen-Thirties." *Hispania,* IX (1926), 1-12.

ALARCÓN, PEDRO ANTONIO DE. "La Desvergüenza." *Obras completas,* 2ª ed., pp. 1782-85. Madrid: Ediciones Fax, 1954.

ALLEN, RUPERT. "The Romantic Element in *Muérete ¡y verás!*" *Hispanic Review,* XXXIV (1966), 218-27. Argues that *Muérete* is an "essential Romantic world view" in Moratinian clothing.

ALONSO CORTÉS, NARCISO. *Bretón de los Herreros, Teatro.* Madrid: Espasa-Calpe, 1943. Contains a succinct prologue by a well-known scholar.

ASENSIO, JOSÉ MARÍA. "El Teatro de Don Manuel Bretón de los Herreros." *La España Moderna* (Madrid), XCVII (1897), 79-100.

BLASCO, EUSEBIO. "Las costumbres en el teatro: su influencia recíproca." In *La España del Siglo XIX, Curso de 1886-1887,* III, 121-71. *(Ateneo Científico, Literario y Artístico de Madrid).*

BRUNETIÈRE, FERDINAND. *Brunetière's Essays in French Literature.* New York: Scribner's, 1898. Some of his ideas on Molière are applicable to Bretón: see p. 66.

BURGOS, CARMEN DE ("Colombine"). *Fígaro.* Madrid: Imprenta de "Alrededor del Mundo," 1919. See Chapter XIV: "Larra y Bretón."

CALDERÓN, FERNANDO. *A ninguna de las tres.* México: Editorial Porrúa, 1972. A Mexican imitation of Bretón's *Marcela.*

CALDERWOOD, J.L. AND TOLIVER, H.E. *Perspectives in Drama.* (New York: Oxford U. Press, 1968. pp. 163-76 explain the *senex* figure.

CAMPO, AGUSTÍN DEL. "Sobre la *Marcela* de Bretón." *Berceo,* II (1947), 41-55.

CAMPOS, JORGE. *Teatro y sociedad en España, 1780-1820.* Madrid: Editorial Moneda y Crédito, 1969. See pp. 95-108 concerning the middle class in the theater.

CARR, RAYMOND. *Spain, 1808-1939.* Oxford, 1966. An outstanding history of nineteenth century Spain.

CEJADOR Y FRAUCA, JULIO. *Historia de la lengua y literatura castellana,* VI, 405-15. Madrid: Tip. de la Revista de Archivos, 1918.

CERVERA Y JIMÉNEZ-ALFARO, FRANCISCO. "Bretón en el siglo XX y en la intimidad." *Berceo,* II (1947), 11-15.

CHASKIN, SILVIA NOVO BLANKENSHIP. "Social Satire in the Works of Manuel Bretón de los Herreros." Doctoral dissertation, University of Virginia, 1968; Ann Arbor: University Microfilms, 1969. After Molíns's biography of 1883 and Le Gentil's study of 1909, this dissertation is the most complete study of Bretón's theater. Shows the ultimate seriousness of his comedy.

CHAULIÉ, DIONISIO. *Cosas de Madrid. Apuntes sociales de la villa y corte.* Madrid: M.G. Hernández, 1884. See pp. 221-29 and 275-79.

CHAVES, MANUEL. *Bocetos de una época (1820-1840).* Madrid: Librería de Fernando Fe, 1892.

CONSIGLIO, CARLO. "Algunas comedias de Bretón de los Herreros y sus relaciones con Goldoni." *Berceo,* II (1947), 137-45.

COREY, JAMES ALAN. "The Comedies of Manuel Bretón de los Herreros." Doctoral dissertation, UCLA, 1972; Ann Arbor: University Microfilms, 1973.

DÍAZ-PLAJA, FERNANDO. *La vida española en el siglo XIX.* Madrid: Afrodisio Augado, 1952.

DUFFEY, FRANK M. "Juan de Grimaldi and the Madrid Stage (1823-1837)." *Hispanic Review,* X (1942), 147-56.

ESCOBAR, JOSÉ. "Sobre la formación del artículo de costumbres." *Boletín de la Real Academia Española,* 50 (1970), 559-73. Several references to Bretón's *costumbrismo.*

FASTENRATH, JOHANNES. *Lustspiele von Don Manuel Bretón de los Herreros.* Deutsch von Johannes Fastenrath. Dresden: Verlag von Carl Reissner, 1897. The German Hispanophile Fastenrath translated four

of Bretón's plays, namely: *Stirb und Du wirst sehen (Muérete ¡y verás!); Ein weiblicher Don Juan (Una de tantas); Sie ist Er (Ella es él)* and *Der Friedliebender (El hombre pacífico).*
FERRER DEL RÍO, ANTONIO. *Galería de la literatura española,* pp. 127-40. Madrid: Mellado, 1846.
GARCÍA CASTAÑEDA, SALVADOR. "Juan Martínez Villergas y un cuadro de Esquivel." *Revista de Estudios Hispánicos* (Alabama), VII (1973), 179-92. Explains the attacks of Villergas on Bretón.
GARCÍA LORENZO, LUCIANO. "Bretón y el teatro romántico." *Berceo,* 90 (Enero-Junio 1976), 69-82. Argues that Bretón criticized the abuses of Romanticism but not Romanticism itself. Cites two of his translations, two of his historical dramas, and *Elena* as evidence.
GARCÍA PRADO, JUSTINIANO. "Bretón y su patria chica." *Berceo,* II (1947), 57-62.
GIL Y ZRATE, ANTONIO. "Don Manuel Bretón de los Herreros." In Nicomedes Pastor Díaz, *Galería de españoles célebres contemporáneos,* pp. 1-53. Madrid: Imprenta de Sánchez, 1841.
GOENAGA, ANGEL, and MAGUNA, JUAN P. *Teatro español del siglo XIX, análisis de obras.* Long Island City: Las Américas, 1972. Contains a forty page analysis of *Die And You Shall See!*
INGLIS, HENRY DAVID. *Spain.* 2 vols. London: Whittaker, 1837. The second and revised edition of *Spain in 1830.*
IRAVEDRA, LUISA. "Las figuras femeninas del teatro de Bretón." *Berceo,* II (1947), 17-24.
JOSÉ PRADES, JUANA DE. "El teatro de Lope de Vega en los años románticos." *Revista de literatura,* XVIII (1960), 235-48.
KENNEDY, JAMES. *Modern Poets and Poetry of Spain.* London: Longman, Brown, 1852. Contains translations of several poems by Bretón.
LARRA, FERNANDO JOSÉ DE. *La sociedad española a través del teatro del siglo XIX.* Madrid: Ministerio de Trabajo, 1947.
LE GENTIL, GEORGES. *Le Poète Manuel Bretón de los Herreros et la Société Espagnole de 1830 à 1860.* Paris: Hachette, 1909. Le Gentil is the dean of all Bretonian critics.
LESLIE, JOHN KENNETH. *Ventura de la Vega and the Spanish Theatre, 1820-1865.* Princeton, N.J.: University Press, 1940.
LINCOLN, J. N. "A Note of the Indebtedness of Pereda's *La Puchera* to Bretón's *La Independencia.*" *Hispanic Review,* XI (1943), 260-63.
LÓPEZ SERRANO, MATILDE. "Comienzos de Bretón como bibliotecario." *Berceo,* II (1947), 7-9.
LORENZ, CHARLOTTE M. "Translated Plays in Madrid Theatres (1808-1818)." *Hispanic Review,* IX (1941), 376-82.
LOVETT, GABRIEL. "Francophobia in Nineteenth Century Spanish Literature." *Kentucky Romance Quarterly,* XIX (1972), 285-99. Discusses Bretón's *Un francés en Cartagena.*
MARTÍNEZ RUIZ, JOSÉ ("Azorín"). "Los Hermanos Quintero." In *La*

Farándula. In *Obras completas,* VII, 1181-82. Madrid; Aguilar, 1962. Ranks the Quinteros higher than Bretón.

———. *Los Quinteros y otras páginas.* In *Obras completas,* IV, 624-26. Madrid: Aguilar, 1961. Makes a favorable judgement of Bretón.

———. *Rivas y Larra.* In *Obras completas,* III, 485-516. Madrid: Aguilar, 1961. Has a low opinion of Breton.

MARTÍNEZ VILLERGAS, JUAN. *Juicio crítico de los poetas españoles contemporáneos,* pp. 24-28. Paris: Librería de Rosa y Bouret, 1954. An important insight concerning the criticism of Bretón.

MAZADE, CHARLES DE. "La comédie moderne en Espagne: Bretón de los Herreros, Ventura de la Vega, Rodríguez Rubí." *Revue des Deux Mondes* (Paris), XIX (1847), 432-61.

MENÉNDEZ PELAYO, MARCELINO. *Antología General de Menéndez Pelayo,* II, 945-46. Madrid: Biblioteca de Autores Cristianos, 1956.

MESONERO ROMANOS, RAMÓN DE. "Los autores dramáticos de 1836 a 1843." *La Ilustración Española y Americana,* 15 de septiembre de 1881, p. 151.

MOLÍNS, MARQUÉS DE. *Bretón de los Herreros. Recuerdos de su vida y de sus obras.* Madrid: Imprenta de M. Tello, 1883. The story of Breton by his close friend and fellow academician, Mariano Roca de Togores, Marqués de Molíns. Molíns' biography is what Leon Edel calls "the chronicle life."

———. "Don Manuel Bretón de los Herreros." In P. de Novo y Colson, *Autores dramáticos contemporáneos,* II, 147-62. Madrid: Imprenta de Fortanet, 1882.

MORLEY, S. GRISWOLD. "The Curious Phenomenon of Spanish Verse Drama." *Bulletin Hispanique,* L (1948), 445-62. Should be read at the same time as Bretón's Academy speech.

NERVO, AMADO. "Un tercero en discordia." In *Obras completas,* 4ª ed. I, 476-77. Madrid: Aguilar, 1967.

O'BRIEN, ROBERT. *Spanish Plays in English Translation.* New York: Las Américas, 1963. Lists one translation in English of Bretón, his *Una de tantas (One of many),* translated by Willis K. Jones, *Spanish One-Act Plays in English* (Dallas: Tardy, 1934). I know of no other play by Bretón translated into English.

OÑATE, MARÍA DEL PILAR. *El feminismo en la literatura española,* pp. 209-14. Madrid: Espasa-Calpe, 1938. Discusses Bretón's attitude toward women.

PEERS, E. ALLISON. "Literary Ideas in Spain from 1839 to 1854." *Modern Language Review,* XXI (1926), 44-54.

PIFERRER Y FÁBREGAS, PABLO. *Estudios de crítica.* Barcelona: Diario de Barcelona, 1859. Contains five articles reviewing Bretón's plays.

PIÑEYRO, ENRIQUE. *El romanticismo en España.* Paris: Garnier, 1934. Contains a twenty page essay on Bretón's life and work.

QUALIA, CHARLES BLAISE. "Dramatic Criticism in the Comedies of

Selected Bibliography

Bretón de los Herreros." *Hispania,* XXIV (1941), 71-78.
ROGERS, PAUL PATRICK. "The Drama of Pre-Romantic Spain." *The Romanic Review,* XXII (1930), 315-24.
RUBIO, FEDERICO. *Mis maestros y mi educación.* Madrid: Fernando Fe, 1912. Memoirs concerning the years 1827-1850. A forgotten masterpiece, this work should be republished.
RUIZ RAMÓN, FRANCISCO. *Historia del teatro español,* pp. 440-43. Madrid: Alianza Editorial, 1967.
RUMEAU, A. "Le Théâtre à Madrid à la veille du Romantisme, 1831-1834." In *Hommage à Ernest Martinenche,* pp. 330-46. Paris: Éditions Arbrey, 1939.
SIMÓN DÍAZ, JOSÉ. "El Epistolario." *Berceo,* II (1947), 28-40. Contains nineteen letters concerning Bretón.
_____. "Nuevas fuentes para el estudio de Bretón." *Berceo,* II (1947), 25-40.
SMITH, W.F. "Rodríguez Rubí and the Dramatic Reforms of 1849." *Hispanic Review,* XVI (1948), 311 20.
TAMAYO Y BAUS, MANUEL. *Obras completas.* Madrid: Fax, 1947. On pp. 1160-61 he discusses Bretón's *It's Back To Madrid For Me (A Madrid me vuelvo).*
VALERA, JUAN. *Obras completas,* II, 1272-77. Madrid: Aguilar, 1961.
VEGA, VENTURA DE LA. "Don Manuel Bretón de los Herreros." in *Museo de las Familias,* I (1843), 9-10.
WALLIS, SEVERN TREACKLE. *Spain, Her Institutions, Politics and Public Men.* Boston: Ticknor, Reed and Fields, 1853. See Chapters 9, 19, and 20.

Index

(The works of Bretón de los Herreros are listed under his name)

Adaptations (*Refundiciones*), 17, 21, 128-30
Addison, Joseph, 69
Alarcón, Pedro Antonio de, 79-80
Alonso, Dámaso, 135
Aristarch, 19
Assonance, 27
Athenaeum, 19
Azorín (José Martínez Ruiz), 14

Ballads, 97, 98
Balzac, Honoré, 132
Baroja, Pío, 65, 119
Bergson, Henri, 34, 36, 38
Blanco García, Francisco, 89, 100
Boutet de Monvel, 32, 69
Bretón de los Herreros, Manual: birthdate, 14; death, 22; enters the Royal Academy, 20; experience in the army, 15; loss of left eye, 13, 16; marriage, 20; old age, 21; quarrel with Larra, 19; speech before the Royal Academy, 50-55, 76; superficiality charge, 78-80, 103, 148
WORKS-DRAMA:
Attorney For The Poor, 23
Between A Saintly Man and Woman, 72, 115, 119-20
Birds Of A Feather, 53-55, 130
Bodily Senses, The, 13, 14, 33, 71, 128, 131-32
Country Bumpkin, The, 21, 32, 81, 89-93
Dido, 18
Die And You Will See, 20, 21, 45, 81-89, 90
Don Fernando The Summoned, 103, 107-108

Don Frutos In Belchite, 92-94
Editor Responsible, The, 37-40, 44-48, 69
Elena, 18, 89, 103, 106-107
Extraordinary Means, 115
Fat Man, The, 114-16
Ferry-Girl From Pasajes, The, 15, 21, 81, 94-102
Fiancé And Music, The, 130
Frank And Candid Man, The, 23, 31-32, 33, 34, 37, 43
Gilding The Lie, 23, 30, 31, 53
Girl At The Counter, The, 53, 55
Her Fateful Moment, 61, 65, 66-67
I'm Leaving Madrid, 20
Independence, 15, 53-55, 110, 130
It's Back To Madrid For Me, 23, 26-29, 69
Loners, The, 74
Love's Referee, 23, 61, 62
Marcela, 17, 18, 23, 26, 35, 56-67, 68, 69, 76, 81, 90, 133
Mérope, 18, 129
Never At Ease, 103, 109-110
Newspaper, The, 20, 37, 40-44, 70, 73
One More Coquette, 16, 114, 116-17
Parboiled Fiancé, The, 72
Peaceful Man, The, 115
Phony Education, The, 23, 29, 30
Phrenology And Hypnotism, 115, 117-18
Punch, The, 21, 67
Recluses, The, 69
Romeo And Juliet, 29
School Of Wives, The, 73, 74
Show Me The Woman, 81, 103, 110-13
Sweetheart For The Girl, A, 61, 63-64

Index

This World A Farce, 61, 64, 65-66
Three Bouquets, The, 115
To The Letter, 76
Treat Disdain With Love, 104, 110-13
Trials Of Matrimony, The, 115
Two Nephews, The, 15, 23, 25, 26, 69, 72, 73, 76
Vellido Dolfos, 18, 103, 108-109
Water Over The Dam, 74
What's To Be Is To Be, 103, 109-110
Worthy Woman, The, 130
Young Old Codger, The, 17, 23-25, 53, 131
Youthful Adventures, 72

WORKS-POETRY:
"For The Album Of An Actress," 64, 66
"My Lady," 71, 74
"Philharmonic Mania, The," 18
Poems, 125-28
Satires, 126-27
WORKS-PROSE:
Art Of Declamation, 33, 121, 124
Articles Of Local Color, 121-23
Resumés Of Acts And Deeds, 121
Scattered Works, 123-24
"Stone Marriage, The," 14
Bretón y Orozco, Cándido, 20
Brunetière, Ferdinand, 101

Calderón de la Barca, Pedro, 50, 59, 62, 79, 80, 129
Cánovas del Castillo, Antonio, 45
Carlism, 20, 66
Carnerero, José María, 19
Censorship, 33-49
Cervantes, Miguel de, 50, 70, 71, 77, 79
Chaskin, Silvia Novo, 81, 86
Coloma, Luis, 65
Commedia dell'arte, 56, 58
Coquette, 26, 58
Coquetry, 68-80
Corey, James Alan, 84
Covarrubias, Sebastián de, 70
Cruz, Ramón de la, 89, 129

Don Quixote, 30
Donoso Cortés, Juan, 104, 105
Dumas, Alexander, 81

Escosura, Patricio de la, 19
Espronceda, José de, 19, 88, 106-107

Ferdinand VII, 15, 16, 30, 33
Fernán Caballero, 65, 132
Ferrer del Río, Antonio, 78, 79
Figure (talle), 25, 26, 68-80, 95, 96, 97, 133
Frías, Duque de, 19
Frye, Northrop, 23

Gallantry, 68, 80
Gallicisms, 24
García Gutiérrez, Antonio, 106, 107
Gaspar, Enrique, 133
Gil y Carrasco, Enrique, 106
Grimaldi, Juan de, 19, 131

Hartzenbusch, Juan Eugenio, 81, 82, 89, 106, 107, 111, 131
High comedy (alta comedia), 18, 25, 55
Horace, 34, 35, 135
Hugo, Victor, 95, 96, 107, 128

Inglis, Henry David, 75, 117

Jerome, St., 30
Jews in Spain, 84
Juvenal, 65

Lafuente, Modesto, 135
Larra, Mariano José de, 19, 20, 30, 61, 104, 106, 129
Le Gentil, Georges, 62, 68, 81, 121, 128, 134
Lista, Alberto, 19, 20, 50, 127
Local color articles (costumbrismo), 14, 16, 28
Lombía, Juan, 90
López de Ayala, Adelardo, 25, 30, 63
Lyceum, 19

Marivaux, Pierre, 17, 68, 69, 128
Martíinez de la Rosa, Francisco, 106, 129
Martínez Villergas, Juan, 79
Mazade, Charles de, 83, 134
Menéndez Pelayo, Marcelino, 78, 81, 111
Menéndez Pidal, Ramon, 97, 98

Meredith, George, 34, 38
Mesonero Romanos, Ramón, 86, 105
Metrical scheme, 87
Middle class, 15, 16
Molière, 17, 29, 85, 102, 123, 128
Molíns, Marqués de (Mariano Roca de Togores), 19, 20, 21, 50, 61, 81, 82, 84, 107, 114, 125
Moralizing attitude, 30
Moratín, Leandro Fernández de, 17, 24, 26, 27, 29, 36, 37, 53, 54, 60, 61, 63, 69, 80, 105, 106, 123, 124, 129, 133
Moreto, Agustín, 37, 52, 59, 66, 111, 129
Muñoz Seca, Pedro, 89
Nervo, Amado, 62
Newspapers: *Abeja*, 19, 41, 123; *Boletín de comercio*, 19, 41, 123; *Correo literario y mercantil*, 18, 19, 51, 110, 123; *Eco del comercio*, 89
Nineteenth century critics and criticism, 62, 78-80, 101-102, 103
Nineteenth century, judgement of, 32
Novella, 119, 120

Old Christian, 29
Ovid, 50

Palacio Valdés, Armando, 122
Palma, Ricardo, 79, 80
Pardo Bazán, Emilia, 114
Parody, 88, 89, 106
Pereda, José María de, 64, 122
Pérez Galdós, Benito, 65, 132, 133
Pezuela, Juan de la (Conde de Cheste), 19, 68, 127
Piñeyro, Enrique, 100
Poetasters, 26
Príncipe, Miguel Agustín, 90

Quel, 14
Quevedo, Francisco de, 80-82, 111, 112, 113
Quintana, Manuel, 20, 129

Racine, Jean Baptiste, 17, 128
Raisonneur, 25, 30, 31

Rivas, Duque de, 80, 88, 106
Rojas Zorrilla, Francisco de, 59, 69, 92, 93
Romantic comedy, 89
Romanticism, 18, 82, 88, 89, 104-106
Royal Academy of Language, 20, 22, 50
Rueda, Lope de, 51
Ruiz de Alarcón, Juan, 37, 52, 59, 129

Sardoodledum, 64, 115
Sardou, Victorian, 79
Scandal, 25
Scribe, Augustin Eugène, 63, 81, 110, 123, 128
Senex, 23, 24, 27, 40, 133
Serra, Narciso, 33
Shaw, George Bernard, 64
Social customs, 25

Tamayo y Baus, Manuel, 25, 30, 55, 63, 65, 79, 104, 105, 129, 131, 133
Tirso de Molina, 59, 69, 129
Tragedy, 18, 129
Translations, 128-30

Unamuno, Miguel de, 65
Unities, 27

Valera, Juan, 103, 125
Valle-Inclán, Ramón del, 65
Vaudeville, 154
Vega, Ventura de la, 19, 68, 105, 111, 123, 125, 127, 129
Vega y Carpio, Lope de, 37, 50, 53, 59, 69, 83, 129, 133
Versification, 50-55, 58-59, 87
Vis cómica, 13

Wallis, Severn Treackle, 40
Well-made play, 63, 79
Widow (*viudita*), 25
Word padding (*ripios*), 26

Zarzuelas (musical dramas), 129-30
Zoilus, 19
Zorrilla, José, 114, 131